Heart of
Hill Walks

John Newson

Meridian Books

Published 1996 by Meridian Books

© John Newson 1996

ISBN 1-869922-30-1

Meridian Books
40 Hadzor Road, Oldbury, Warley, West Midlands B68 9LA

Printed in Great Britain by BPC Wheatons, Exeter

Contents

Publishers' Note

Every care has been taken in the preparation of this book. All the walks have been independently checked and are believed to be correct at the time of publication. However, no guarantee can be given that they contain no errors or omissions and neither the publishers nor the author can accept responsibility for loss, damage, injury or inconvenience resulting from the use of this book.

Please remember that the countryside is continually changing: hedges and fences may be removed or re-sited; footbridges and river banks may suffer from flood damage; landmarks may disappear; footpaths may be re-routed or ploughed over and not reinstated (as the law requires); concessionary paths may be closed. If you do encounter any such problems the publishers would be very pleased to have details.

Using this book

THE walks in this book range from 10½ to 14½ miles, but most include the option of a shorter walk of between 6 and 10 miles. Some feature fairly modest ascents; others involve fairly steep hill climbs and undulating terrain.

The sketch maps accompanying each walk are intended to serve as guidance and not as replacements for the appropriate Ordnance Survey maps which should always be carried. Even though you may not always need to use them they are, of course, invaluable if in emergency, bad weather or other reason you wish to cut short or re-route your walk. The appropriate numbers of the Landranger (1:50,000) and Pathfinder (1:25,000, with much greater detail) are given in the introduction box at the start of each walk, where you will also find grid references for the starting and finishing points, together with other useful information.

Always carry a compass, have good footwear, preferably good quality walking boots, adequate waterproofs and spare warm clothing. A basic first aid kit should also be carried. Although the introduction box lists pubs and other sources of refreshment it is advisable to carry some food and drink – this can give you some extra independence.

All the walks are circular and for some, public transport being what it is in many rural areas, a car is necessary to reach the starting point. However, some are possible using train or bus and in these cases details are given in the information box. Details of public transport services can be obtained from:

British Rail	0121-643 2711
Gloucestershire	01452-425543
Hereford & Worcester	01905-766800
Shropshire	01345-056785
Staffordshire	01785-223344
West Midlands	0121-200 2700

Introduction

HILLS, whether well known ranges such as the Malverns or the Cotswolds, or more modest mounds, can give walks a focal point, probably their best views, and in some cases provide a minor challenge. A strenuous climb is usually rewarded with a fine view of the surrounding countryside.

These walks explore many of the hills in the Heart of England, from the high open moorlands of Staffordshire in the north, to the remote hills of Shropshire in the west; then south to include Hereford and Worcester's high places, taking in the magnificent Malverns, the great plateau of Bredon, and many lesser known but very scenic hilltops including Oyster Hill, Romsley Hill and the hill on which Hanbury's fine church stands.

Warwickshire's historic Edge Hill and Ilmington Down, its highest point, are featured and going further south some of the hills that make up Gloucestershire's superb Cotswolds are explored.

The Heart of England is well endowed with a great variety of villages built of different materials in differing styles, and a few small towns of character that form an integral part of these walks.

The county of Hereford and Worcester is an administrative combination of the two former shires which became joined as a result of a shot-gun marriage in the local government reorganisation of 1974 and extends from the fringes of Birmingham to the Welsh border. This large county of rolling countryside and inspiring hills, and of orchards and hopyards, has many villages that display fine black and white architecture, with some of the best examples at Elmley Castle, Bosbury and Chaddesley Corbett. The picturesque market town of Ledbury, nestling below the Malverns, has a large number of such buildings.

Warwickshire too has much interesting architecture of which the small historic town of Henley-in-Arden is an outstanding example. It has a long main street of buildings in various styles built since the fifteenth century including some distinctive black and white timbering for which the timbers were obtained from the once surrounding Forest of Arden. Lias, a form of limestone, is featured in Shakespeare country at Aston Cantlow, Binton and Welford-on-Avon. Although Welford has expanded as a ribbon development of modern houses along the main road the heart of the village around the parish church remains a chocolate box picture of lovely old thatched cottages.

Staffordshire has a largely flat and uninspiring terrain and because of this is often considered to be scenically the 'Cinderella' of the Heart of England. However, there are some visually rewarding landscapes as the walks in this county will demonstrate. Some of its villages, such as Alrewas and Barton-under-Needwood, have expanded into small towns to accommodate commuters but have, nevertheless, retained an attractive rural heart. The county's more northern villages, Butterton, Grindon and Waterfall, are situated in a landscape which although administratively in Staffordshire is physically more akin to neighbouring Derbyshire with its hilly terrain and high windswept moorlands.

The character of the Cotswolds, which are largely in Gloucestershire, is founded on oolite limestone which formed its landscape of rolling hills and valleys: it has also created homes for wildlife and encouraged the growth of its profusion of beech trees, and has fashioned its agricultural land for crop growing and its pastures for sheep grazing. Sheep first made the Cotswolds wealthy on wool and cloth in the Middle Ages. Such wealth is now evident in the legacy of many impressive churches and substantial houses which blend with the simpler but equally attractive cottages which are all at one with their glorious surroundings.

The walks pass through some of the lesser known villages, generally well away from tourist honeypots. Guiting Power, in the Windrush Valley, epitomises a traditional Cotswold village with well maintained stone buildings and well stocked colourful gardens in a neat harmony around its sloping village green. Smaller, but also beautifully unspoilt, are Wyck Rissington, Icomb and Hazleton which have a quiet and mellow serenity where time seems to stand still. Compton Abdale is deep in a dale and Cold Aston is high on the wold.

More remote are the upland villages of South Shropshire with Wentnor and Minton set in idyllic countryside around the Long Mynd. A little to the south is the quartet of villages by the River Clun – Clun, Clunton, Clunbury and Clungunford – which are well known for being, as Housman described them, 'the quietest places under the sun'. Surely there is still much truth in this as the countryside is unspoilt, large towns are non-existent, main roads are insignificant and motorways have thankfully not yet reached this fine border country, west of Ludlow, which is far from the madding crowd ...

Location Map

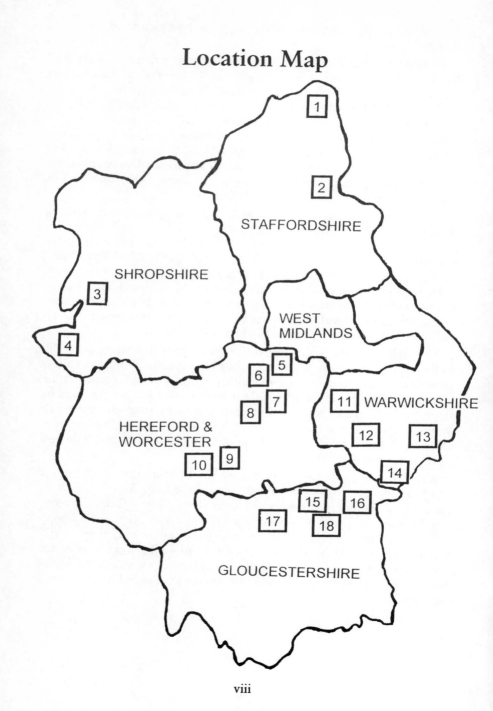

1

Butterton and the Hill

This walk visits the high villages of Butterton, Ford, Grindon and Waterfall and climbs steeply to the 'Hill' for fine views over the Staffordshire Moorlands. It also has some interesting water features including some pleasant meetings with the River Hamps.

Distance: 12 or 9 miles
Maps: Landranger 119; Outdoor Leisure Map 24
Car Parking: Lay-by at Onecote Church
Start/Finish: Onecote (GR049552)
Refreshments: Pubs: Butterton, Grindon and Waterfall
Shorter Version: This walk can be shortened to 9 miles by taking the lane from Grindon direct to Ford.

! There are two fords on this walk (at GR075562 and GR083519) that may prove difficult to cross after heavy and prolonged rain.

FROM Onecote Church walk north along Bradnop Lane for a quarter of a mile, then fork right on a bridle-way passing between the buildings of Onecote Grange. This bridle-way is a wide track running parallel with the River Hamps until it reaches, in 1¼ miles, Mixon Mine Farm. Ignoring a footpath sign to Butterton go through the farmyard and bear right on a path signed 'Mermaid'and shortly bear left up a slope to follow a clear path north over further stiles for half a mile until the path, now a track, swings left to pass two old stone gateposts. Here turn right and descend the meadow along a somewhat indistinct path to the River Hamps, cross by the footbridge and ascend the steep slope straight ahead through three fields to a lane on the summit of the hill.

Turn left along the lane until you reach a stile on the right: cross this and go up to the trig point on 'The Hill' (1394 ft). There are rewarding views from here including the stately church spires of Butterton and

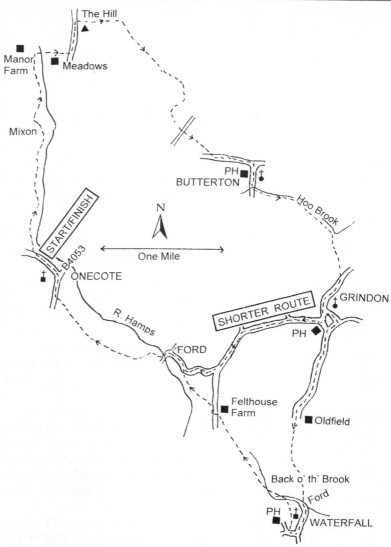

Grindon to the east and the dominant feature of the Morridge ridge to the west.

After absorbing the panorama go straight ahead and descend steeply, crossing two stiles to reach a farm track to the left of a house named 'Under the Hill'. Almost immediately cross a stile on the left of the track and descend, bearing right across a field to a footbridge. Climb a steep slope with a fence on the left and continue to Ryecroft. Here go straight ahead, left of the farm, and then bear right, to cross a stile and a footbridge by pine trees and, keeping a hedge/fence on the left, follow the path to New Hole Farm (shown as 'Hole' on the OS map). Walk past the house and outbuildings and turn left along a track: then turn right to take a signed path which contours around the slope, and then go up a narrow gulley (hedge on left, fence on right) to Hill Farm. There are wide views from this path across the moorlands.

From Hill Farm take the track to the right for about 20 yards, then take a signed path on the left that shortly emerges on a track which descends, then ascends to the B5053. Cross the road and take the path immediately opposite through five fields, aiming for the spire of Butterton church. Emerging in Butterton walk through the village to the Black Lion inn, opposite the church.

The name 'Butterton' is probably derived from 'butter town' meaning an enclosure where cows were kept and butter was made.

From the Black Lion inn descend the lane and round a bend to the ford. Continue on this lane for about 100 yards. Go through a squeeze stile beside a gate, then immediately cross a wooden stile on the left and take a path on the left that bears down the slope to Hoo Brook. Follow the path alongside the right bank of the brook for about a mile until a junction of tracks is reached. Here turn right by the National Trust sign to take the bridle-way that climbs through four meadows to reach a lane.

Turn right on the lane and in a quarter of a mile arrive at Grindon. The name Grindon stems from 'Grendon' meaning green hill which aptly describes the site of this village in its elevated position on the moorlands overlooking the Manifold Valley. It has been described as 'one of those high places which, as if being drawn towards it, seem to have more than its share of the sky'.

From the picnic site by the church continue along the lane and then turn left to reach the village. At the next fork turn right, then right again at the T-junction. After walking 150 yards reach another junction at the Cavalier Inn.

If you wish to take the shortened route turn right at the Cavalier Inn and soon go first left. After just over a quarter of a mile turn left and then left again at the following junction. When the next T-junction is reached go straight on along the lane to the hamlet of Ford. Now continue reading from ✱ on page 4.

Continuing on the main route turn left at the inn and continue along this lane for a mile, passing Summerhill Farm, to reach Oldfield. Here the lane becomes a track which should be followed for three quarters of a mile (the track becomes a path at one stage) until a road is reached at Back o' th' Brook. Go straight ahead across the ford and up the steep lane to the T-junction at the top, then take the lane to the right which leads to the hamlet of Waterfall.

Take a path right, beside a telephone box, that leads in a few yards to Waterfall Church. With the churchyard on the right and tall trees on the left, walk through meadowland to reach a stile beside a large ash tree. Then bear left across the next field to a footbridge where the brook has become a pool.

Cross the bridge and go over a wall stile to a lane and turn left. In about 120 yards, at a junction, take the right fork: continue along this for a quarter of a mile, then, immediately after passing a brook take a faint path to the left (unsigned at the time of writing), bearing slightly right to climb a bank and cross a stile into a field.

Keeping on the same heading (NNW) across three fields, ford a brook and make for a house across on the far side of the field (Felthouse Farm). Cross the road at the farm and walk through the yard and between barns to take a path to the right immediately after passing the barns.

Go over a stile, and forward to another stile, then go down a steep bank and through a broken gate onto a track. Turn left and continue until a farm is reached. Go right through iron gates just before a cattle grid, keeping right of barns.

The path is on a raised bank alongside the River Hamps for a few yards until a bridge and stile are reached. After the stile walk straight ahead to soon meet the river again on the left. Cross a stile and go forward along a track which, after passing a gate on the right, becomes a path with a fence on the right. After crossing another stile the fence becomes a hedge and the path meets a track.

Go through a squeeze stile and turn left along a lane to reach Ford village.

✶ *Continue from here if you have taken the shorter route.*

Go through the village where, over a bridge, turn right, taking the lane which is clearly defined for about half a mile when, at Ford Wetley House, it becomes a path. Maintain the same heading, passing Clough House Farm, where the path becomes a lane to the B5053. At the road turn right for a quarter of a mile and turn left and return to your starting point, Onecote Church.

2

Alrewas and Battlestead Hill

Rising from a ridge in the Needwood Forest, Battlestead Hill has a vista across the Trent Valley. The walk also includes the villages of Barton and Tatenhill, passes the remains of the medieval village of Wychnor, and commences at Alrewas which is situated at the junction of the River Trent and the Trent and Mersey Canal. The presence of these waterways greatly adds to the appeal of this village which has some fine sixteenth century black and white thatched houses in its main street. The name Alrewas, a corruption of 'Alder Wash', refers to the alder trees that once grew nearby in the Trent flood plain and gave rise to the basket weaving for which the village was once well-known.

Distance: 14½ miles or 9 miles or 12 miles
Maps: Landranger 128; Pathfinder 852/872
Car Parking: Alrewas (streetsides)
Public Transport: Bus; Stephenson's 112
(Birmingham-Lichfield-Alrewas-Burton upon Trent). Alight in Alrewas at the George and Dragon. NB *There is a very limited service from Birmingham so if you are travelling from here it is probably better to take the train to Lichfield. From Lichfield there is a more regular 112 service to Alrewas and Burton.*
Start/Finish: Alrewas War Memorial (GR171151)
Refreshments: Pubs in Alrewas, Tatenhill and Barton-under-Needwood
Shortened Version: The walk can be shortened to 9 miles by eliminating the northern section beyond Dunstall. Alternatively it can be shortened to 12 miles by finishing at Barton-under-Needwood and returning from there by the Stevenson's 112 bus to Alrewas or Lichfield.

FROM the war memorial in Alrewas Main Street go down Post Office Road and turn left into Church Lane and over the canal bridge. Go right along the towpath and shortly cross a long trestle bridge. Looking to the left from here Alrewas presents a very tranquil scene with

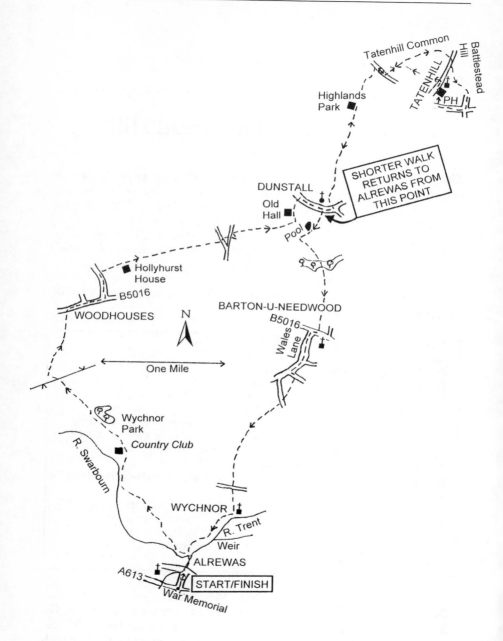

the parish church above the willows and the placid waters of the River Trent and the millstream in the foreground.

Turn left at the end of the trestle bridge on a signed path which bears left across a field to a track. Cross the track and take a path opposite straight across the middle of the field (the old hedge, part way across this field, is not now the field boundary). Go through a gap in the far hedge to bear right (north) in a second field. Cross a stream to bear left in a third field and soon walk with the River Swarbourn on the left.

Cross another stream (bridge stile) and go straight across a small meadow to reach a bank of trees. Here go left briefly and then right to climb the bank and go left across the parkland (golf course – beware flying missiles!) to a stile in front of Wychnor Country Club. Go straight ahead on a driveway for about 250 yds and take a path on the left.

Walk forward (bearing 310 degrees) to woodland, cross a stile and follow a path at the edge of the woodland for just over a quarter of a mile until a rough track is reached; here bear right over a stile and then soon over another stile to enter a narrow strip of woodland. Bear right on a waymarked path to a stile and turn left to walk with woodland on the left.

Descend a slope, cross a stream and ascend the next field; go through a second field and make for the pylon line. Go under this to reach a lane and turn right along this. After three-quarters of a mile a junction is reached: turn right on a road (B5016) and take the second lane (Sich Lane) on the left for about 250 yds. Just before Round Cottage turn right through a gate on a path with a hedge on the right.

Go through a second gate, then cross a stile to pass farm buildings (Hollyhurst House). Very shortly cross another stile, then go straight forward (hedge on right) to a fence stile. Cross this and go forward toward a large tree with a pylon in the distance behind it. Cross a fence stile to the right of the tree, then go straight forward to a step stile. Now continue forward over several more stiles to pass a pylon and reach a lane. Here turn left for a few yards and then take a path on the right straight across a field to another lane.

Turn left and take the second signposted path (signed Dunstall ¾) on the right. The path goes on a well defined track through trees to emerge in parkland with good views of Dunstall's Victorian Church.

At a junction of tracks go left to pass the Old Hall to a lane and turn right and after just over a quarter of a mile reach Dunstall church.

If you are following the shorter walk now continue reading from ✳ *on page 8.*

A little beyond Dunstall church turn left at a signed bridleway. The track passes Sprinks Barn Farm and continues straight on as a bridleway to

Highlands Park, then beyond on a metalled lane to cottages on a bend. Continue on the lane and shortly, when a junction is reached, turn right. Then soon turn left down Cuckoo Cage Lane and follow this metalled lane for about half a mile until a gate is reached at Lingbourne Stud. Here continue straight ahead on the wide track which is a pleasant ridge walk: Collingwood Hall can be seen across to the left.

At the third gate the obvious track ends: here continue walking on a slightly sunken green track with a hedge on the right. When the hedge bends to the right go left across the open field and descend the slope to Tatenhill, following waymarks to a stile between the stream and a cottage, and onto a lane. Cross the lane and take the path opposite, bearing right up the slope and then straight ahead along a line of telegraph poles towards woodland, with the village on the right.

When the wood is reached go over a stile (waymarked 'Battlestead and Back') and bear right on the path to its highest point in the wood. Battlestead Hill (295 ft) is reputed to be the site of a battle between the Angles and the Danes. The woodland is in the care of the Woodland Trust. Continue walking by taking the right-hand fork down to a stile and gate.

From here there are views across the Trent Valley and to the beer town of Burton-upon-Trent with the all too obvious cooling towers of its power station. Descend the hill, walking with a narrow strip of woodland on the right to a road and turn right (at boarding kennels). After about half a mile turn right on a path beside a large rock of mudstone (*Keuper marl*). The path continues with a stream on the left and soon goes straight across a field to emerge on a drive at Mill House. Turn left and climb the drive to the lane in Tatenhill, then turn right to the parish church.

Tatenhill is a most attractive village situated in a hollow between the gentle rounded hills of the Tatenhill Ridge, and has some notable buildings including the parish church dating from the thirteenth century and a substantial Georgian rectory.

Immediately opposite the church take the path (signed Tatenhill Common). Walk up the field and then go through a gate to walk on the same heading with a hedge on the right through the next field. Then go straight across a third field and then along a hedged way to reach Cuckoo Cage Lane (met earlier on the walk). Turn left and at the junction turn right for a few yards (passing a phone box) and then turn left at the next junction. Soon cottages on the right are reached and from here retrace your outward steps for 1½ miles back to Dunstall Church.

✶ *Continue reading from here if you are following the shorter walk.*

Take the path beside a cattle grid opposite the church along an avenue of oak trees and past a pool. After half a mile, and just before cottages, a

Barton-under-Needwood. The Churchyard

junction of tracks will be reached: here turn left through a hunter's gate and ascend a field bearing left to go left of a pylon and through gates in the fence to go across a field towards woodland, and then over a stile through the wood. Emerging from the wood descend the field (Smith Hills) bearing slightly left on a clear bridleway to a gate. Maintain the same heading across a second field to reach a stile in the far left corner.

Now turn right and walk with a fence on the left in a third field; then along a gravel drive to the road (B5016). Turn left to Barton-under-Needwood village centre.

The name Barton probably stems from 'Barley Town', meaning a place where barley or any form of grain was stored. It still has an old village nucleus with attractive cottages and Georgian houses around its parish church, in spite of being swollen by newer developments into a small town. The wooded churchyard is a delight.

To resume the walk return to the Red Lion and turn off the main road (B5016) at Wales Lane; go down this lane and The Green to turn left into Captains Lane. After a few yards turn right over a stile onto a path across a field. Cross a stream in the far left corner and then walk with the stream on the right for a 100 yards to a lane: here turn left. Very shortly turn right along a track (signed Green Lane) for a mile to reach a lane.

Approaching the lane you may be fortunate enough to see an old Theakston's brewery dray in the field. Shire horses are bred nearby and taken around the country on promotions for the brewery.

At the crossroads go straight ahead to Wychnor Church, passing the Midlands Equestrian Centre. The remains of the medieval village of Wychnor (a scheduled Ancient Monument, in the care of English Heritage) can be seen in the fields to the right as you approach the church. Just before the church go right through a hunter's gate onto a path which goes diagonally down to the towpath of the Trent & Mersey Canal.

Turn right and take the towpath back to Alrewas. You will soon pass a weir – something that you do not normally expect to see on a canal. The explanation lies in the link here between the Trent & Mersey Canal and the River Trent which in this area share the waterway for some 200 yards. You will meet this link a little further ahead where the towpath crosses the waterway by the long trestle bridge met earlier on the walk. Approaching Alrewas look out for the fine 1819 iron canal mile post.

3

The Long Mynd

The Long Mynd, Shropshire's bleak and lonely ridge, and its spur Adstone Hill, give an exhilarating walk in Border Country. The route includes the upland villages of Wentnor and Minton. The latter is an ancient settlement dating from Saxon times and could have been a frontier settlement of Mercia.

Distance: 12½ miles or 8 miles
Maps: Landranger 137; Pathfinder 909/910
Car Parking: Roadsides in Minton or Asterton
Public Transport (*adds 1½ miles*): Midland Red West 435 (Ludlow-Shrewsbury). Alight at Marshbrook and walk NW for about three quarters of a mile along the minor road to Minton
Start/Finish: Minton (GR429908) or Asterton (GR398912)
Refreshments: Pub, Wentnor
Shortened Version: The walk may be shortened to 8 miles by starting/finishing at Asterton (GR398912) eliminating the Minton section. Start reading from ✱ on page 12.

S TARTING from Minton Green turn right (west) at the telephone box along a narrow lane for a quarter of a mile and then take an easily missed signed bridleway on the right, a few yards past a metal gate on the right. This very soon goes through a gate and contours around the edge of the hill to a track where you turn right for a few yards and then go left over a bridge. The track then climbs steeply: after a few yards, when reaching a house on the right, leave the track and go straight up along a bridlepath through trees.

On reaching a gate on the left turn right to go up the shoulder of a steep hill, passing under power lines. Keeping on the same heading go through a gate and along a track coming in from the left to walk through conifer woods, ignoring a branch to the right. When the track emerges from the woods go straight ahead for just under half a mile and turn right at a gate along a wide track on the edge of the hill. After about a quarter of a mile

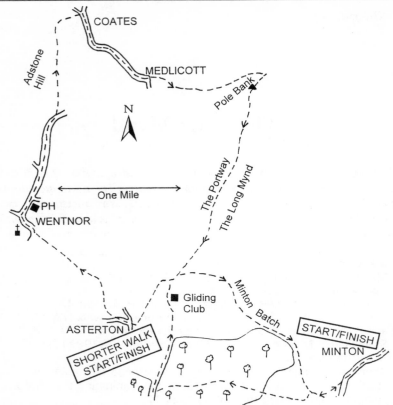

take the permissive path signed Starboardway (no prizes for working out the significance of this name!) which forks to the left to go past the gliding club buildings.

Just beyond the club reach a narrow lane.

Turn left along the lane which descends steeply to the hamlet of Asterton. There are excellent views from here westwards to Wentnor and the Welsh hills.

✳ *Start here for the shorter walk. From Asterton walk along the lane going west.*

When the lane reaches a junction go right for a few yards and then turn left at the next junction. After about 150 yards go right up a track for about another 150 yards and then through a gate. Keeping the same heading, with a hedge/fence on the right, cross a stream and then bear slightly left to a fence stile in the far hedge; then continue bearing left across the next field to cross a bridge stile. Keep on the same heading in the next large field to some oak trees in the far left-hand corner. Then cross a fence stile and walk with a fence on the right for a few yards to cross a stile and bridge over Criftin Brook.

Ascend the meadow, bearing right to a fence, and then walk with this fence on the right to a lane and turn right to reach Wentnor Church, then go right to walk through the village, passing (or visiting) the Crown Inn.

When the buildings cease carry on along the same heading along the narrow lane for about three quarters of a mile where the lane bears right. Here go ahead on a track that climbs to Adstone Hill. Continue by descending the hill on a tree lined track which after a quarter of a mile curves to the right to a cluster of buildings at Coates.

Turn right just past a bungalow onto a metalled track which is followed as it twists and turns for about a mile to the small settlement at Medlicott. Here go straight on along the steep track, metalled as far as a cottage, then unsurfaced, up the Long Mynd. In about three quarters of a mile this reaches a junction of tracks at Pole Bank, signed 'The Jack Mytton Way' on the left but, at the time of writing, unsigned on the right.

Go right through a traffic barrier of four posts to shortly reach a trig point and a toposcope at a height of 1696 ft with more fine views – the area is best visited when the heather is in bloom. This bridlepath is named in memory of 'Mad Jack' Mytton , a skilled horseman who was apparently a drunken but likeable rogue, and was at one time MP for Shrewsbury and died at the tender age of 37.

Continue on this bridleway until a lane is reached – this is the ancient track known as the Portway, a medieval track running for ten miles along the Long Mynd. Turn right and proceed along this metalled track, passing tracks on the left to Little Stretton and Minton until a junction of tracks (met earlier in the walk) is reached.

For the shorter walk continue forward, soon passing the Gliding Club on the left and descending to your starting point of Asterton.

Continuing the longer walk turn left by the National Trust sign and walk across the rough ground and then descend on the path, with a fence on the right, through the lovely Minton Batch for approximately 1½ miles until farm buildings are reached on the right. Minton Batch is an especially scenic and peaceful part of the Long Mynd where A E Housman's words come to mind:

> *Across the glittering pastures and empty upland still*
> *And solitude of shepherds high in the folded hill*

At the farm buildings branch left through a gate (left of a cattle grid) to follow the bridleway and lane, retracing your outward steps back to Minton.

4

The Cluns

Situated in the peaceful Shropshire countryside, the villages of Clunbury, Clunton, Clungunford and Clun are supposed to be the 'quietest places under the sun'. This ramble includes three of the Cluns together with a saunter along the River Clun, and attains the height of Bury Ditches.

Distance: 12 miles or 8½ miles
Maps: Landranger 137; Pathfinder 930
Car Parking: Lanes at Kempton (off B4385)
Start/Finish: Kempton (GR361830)
Refreshments: Pubs, Clun, Clunton and Purslow; Café, Clun
Shortened Version: The walk can be shortened to 8½ miles by taking the lane to Clunton after the climb to Bury Ditches Fort.

ON the road (B4385) in Kempton, walking in a northerly direction, turn left (the third turning on the left) along a narrow lane for a short distance and then take a path on the right (part of the Shropshire Way) which bears left across a field to an estate road where you turn left. Shortly cross the River Kemp (footbridge). Soon after turn left to bear left on a path across a pasture to emerge on a track at a junction of paths/tracks. Here turn right briefly and then take the left fork along a bridleway through Walcot Park.

After about a mile the path forks left by a cottage and through woods, but parallel to the track, and then emerges to follow the track with woodland on the left. Emerging from the woodland the track swings left; our path goes forward over a stile and past a cottage (Stanley Cottage) with outbuildings and continues to a lane.

At the lane turn right for a few yards and then go left at the car park. Bury Ditches Hill fort was an Iron Age fort with fortifications covering an area of about seven acres and until recently was covered by trees.

From the car park ascend the track past an information board and following the dark green waymark posts to the summit (1274 ft) where

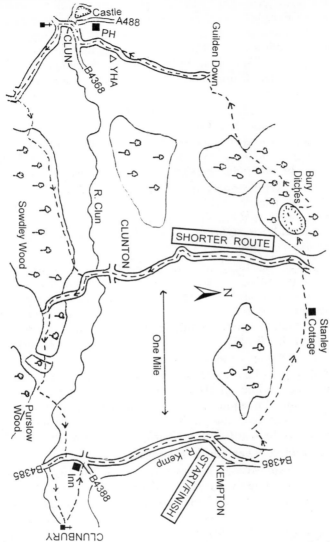

there are far ranging views of the Shropshire Hills. Retrace the last 100 yards of your steps from the toposcope to the track.

If you are doing the shorter walk retace your steps to the car park and turn right at the lane (that you previously walked) and continue for 1¾ miles to the village of Clunton. Cross the main road (B4386) and carry on along the lane southwards from the village; cross the River Clun and climb the steep lane. Now continue reading from ✱ *on page 16*

At the track turn right by the signpost (Forest Walks). Go over a stile by a gate to go right along a wide grassy track. Shortly a junction of tracks is reached (by a seat which has good views north to Bishops Castle): here turn left and follow a track through woodland, ignoring branches off and turning right at a T-junction, for approximately three quarters of a mile until a track signed 'Clun' and marked 'Jack Mytton Way' and 'Shropshire Way' is reached on the left.

Follow this track to farm buildings at Guilden Down and turn left on the lane to Clun for almost three quarters of a mile before taking a path (waymarked Shropshire Way) on the right which bears left across three fields and then down a driveway to rejoin the lane, passing the YHA building, to branch right, then left, then right to reach Clun.

Clun, a small stone town rather than a village, is the largest of the quartet and its notable features include the remains of an early Noman castle, and the parish church that has a fortress-like tower typical of border country. The ancient saddleback bridge, which spans the River Clun, dates from the fourteenth century.

From Clun take the A488 road (signed Knighton) over the ancient bridge and up to the church, turning left at Vicarage Road. At the next junction turn right and climb the lane for approximately half a mile to reach the hamlet of Woodside and, at the second T-junction (by a cottage named Stonewalls) turn left along a track (the left fork of two tracks) and remain on the track which goes straight ahead (ignoring branches off) and soon enters Sowdley Wood.

After about 1¼ miles the track swings right and uphill: here go ahead on a waymarked bridlepath (Jack Mytton Way), soon going through a gate, then continuing for about another a quarter of a mile until a lane is reached. (A slight diversion can be made by turning left here if you want to have a closer look at Clunton.) Turn right to climb the steep lane.

✷ *Continue from here on the shorter walk.*

Go along the lane for approximately a quarter of a mile until a path on the left, signed Clunton Coppice Nature Reserve, through woodland is taken. Follow the waymarks, ignore a branch right and turn left when the track forks.

At Ladye Bank bear left down a track through woods and then on a sunken track to a lane and turn right.

Stay on this lane for about 150 yards and then go left over a stile beside a metal gate. Go down through the centre of a field until reaching a large oak tree. Here swing right to a stile, then go across the corner of the next field to a bridge over the River Clun. Cross this and go across the field to a metal gate in the right-hand hedge/fence. Here go straight forward to pass an ancient ash on the left and to the right of a large house to the road at Purslow (B4385).

Turn right for just under a quarter of a mile and turn left over a stile on a path at the bridge which, firstly, runs parallel to the river on the right and then near its tributary brook through four fields to the footbridge at Clunbury. This is very a picturesque spot with the fine and very 'English' view of Clunbury's cottages and church in front of Clunbury Hill, and the waters of the brook that flow into the Clun river beneath your feet.

Retrace your steps across the footbridge and go diagonally right across the field to the far hedge; here go through a gate and continue on the same heading, now with a hedge and trees on the right in a second field. Shortly cross a stile and then walk with a hedgerow on the left in a third field to reach a gate into the next (fourth) field.

Cross this field diagonally right towards trees in the top right corner. At the corner cross a stile (waymarked) and walk very briefly through pine trees and bear right to go across the garden of a house on the right. Then go through a gate/stile into a small orchard and over a stile to the road (B4368), and turn left to the crossroads.

From the Hundred House Inn turn right to take the long lane back to Kempton. Eventually, after just over a mile, take the right fork which crosses the River Kemp and soon returns you to the B4385 and the end of the ramble which has explored the area described by A E Housman in *A Shropshire Lad*:

> *In the valleys of springs and rivers*
> *By Onny and Teme and Clun*
> *The country for easy livers*
> *The quietest under the sun.*

5

Illey and Waseley Hill

Exploring the countryside to the immediate west of the Birmingham City boundary, this ramble goes via Halesowen Abbey and Illey to gain the heights of Romsley, Windmill and Waseley Hills.

Distance: 12½ miles or 9½ miles
Maps: Landranger 139; Pathfinder 933/953/974
Car Parking: Woodgate Country Park Visitor Centre car park
Public Transport: West Midlands Travel 23
Start/Finish: Woodgate Valley Country Park, Clapgate Lane, Woodgate, Birmingham (GR994829)
Refreshments: Pubs – Romsley, Illey; Café – Waseley Visitor Centre
Place of interest: Halesowen Abbey (English Heritage)
Shortened Version: The walk can be shortened to 9½ miles by starting/finishing at Illey (GR983817). *Very limited roadside parking.* Start reading from ✪ on page 20. NB For public transport users the only practical starting point is Woodgate.

ROM Woodgate Country Park Visitor Centre walk northwards descending a fenced bridleway to a bridge over the Bourne Brook and turn left along a wide track with the brook on the left. Shortly, at a bend, a junction of tracks is reached. Here bear right to follow a path through grassland with houses to the left and the A456 road (Quinton Expressway) to the right for about 250 yards to meet the cul-de-sac of Eldon Road.

Proceed along Eldon Road and shortly, at the T-junction, turn right along Carters Lane to cross the M5 motorway bridge. Just beyond the bridge turn left to go over a stile (signed Lapal) on the left. Walk with a hedge on the right down a sloping field, then bear half left up a rough track and just before farm buildings are reached turn right over a stile and across a field and then down a narrow gully on the left of a large house to a lane at Lapal.

1

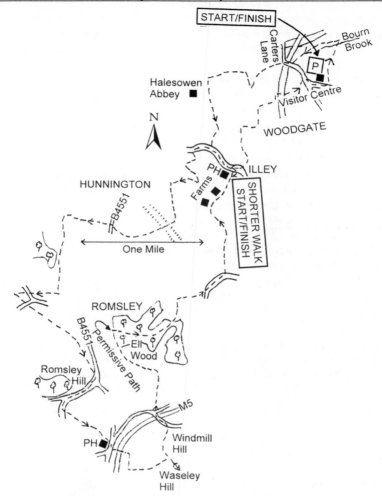

Cross the lane and take a track opposite to reach a house and stables. The track now becomes a path; follow this then turn right where the path splits taking a path with a hedge on the right, descend to the bottom of the field, and then with a hedge on the right walk along the bottom boundary of the field. Continue on the same heading through the next field, and then, after turning right at a stile, walk with a hedge on the left in the following field for approximately 150 yards, noting the remains of the old Abbey fishponds on the right. Turn left over a stile (at a hedge corner) and walk straight across a meadow with a fence on the right.

This historic area was once part of the very large Manor of Hales as recorded in the Domesday Book of 1086. It was then in the hands of Roger de Montgomery, he having been given it by William the Conqueror. Later, in 1177, it passed to David ap Owen, hence the probable origin of the present name of 'Halesowen'.

From here to the right can be seen the remains of Halesowen Abbey which was founded in 1215 as a religious house of the Premonstratensian Order. The monks remained in control of the Manor of Halesowen until the dissolution of the monasteries in 1538. Only one complete building remains – the Infirmary – which can be visited on occasional open days, the site being in the care of English Heritage.

Bear left in the following field for approximately 100 yards, then swing right over a brook, then left (following waymarks), then along a raised path by a right-hand hedge for about a quarter of a mile. Turn right across a field and left at a waymark post in the centre of this large field. Continue to a lane and turn right.

✪ *Start here for the shorter walk. From Illey go west/north-west along the lane to pass the Black Horse on your left.*

Take the next left turn (a farm track) and in about 50 yards turn right over a stile just before farm buildings (Illey Brook Farm) are reached. Go straight down the field to the Illey Brook and turn left to walk with the brook on your right for two fields, then cross the brook a little way past a yellow marker sign to reach a track (adjacent to the gun club grounds). Turn right along this track for about 300 yards – the track then becomes a path with a fence on the right until it reaches a stile on the right.

Go over this stile and turn left to walk through two fields with a hedge on the left; in a third field cross a stream (bridge) to go straight to a signpost

The remains of Halesowen Abbey

on the far boundary. Turn right here to walk with a field on the left. Cross a disused railway track and go straight on to reach the corner of a copse, then swing left across a field and walk with a hedge on the right for about 50 yards before going right across a stile in this hedge. Go straight on up the field, passing to the right of a farm (Hollies Farm) on the left and then head right towards a stile in the far right corner which you cross to reach a road (B4551) in Hunnington.

Turn right down the road for approximately 100 yards and then turn left (next to a white bungalow) along the track which is a public footpath (signed Uffmoor Lane). After approximately 250 yards a crossroads of tracks is reached; here go straight on between farm buildings on the left and a wooden bungalow on the right.

At the end of farm buildings go over a stile and soon over another one to the right of a small pool. Continue straight ahead to a marker post in the middle of the large field and turn left to climb the slope to a stile in the hedge/fence. Then bear left in two fields following clear white and yellow marker posts.

Eventually, when a second pool is reached, walk around the edge of this (with the pool on the right), then bear left of it to follow further clear yellow waymarker posts that go left of woodland. Then go over two stiles only a few yards apart at the edge of a wood. Continue ascending the slope, firstly with a wood on the right, then with a hedge on the right, through two large fields.

At the end of the second field, just before barns are reached, turn right over a stile and walk with a hedge on the left through one field, then bear left through a second to emerge on a lane by a white house (Lyttleton Croft). Cross the lane and go over a stile, then bear right across a large field to another stile in the far hedge. Go straight across a narrow field and turn left to walk with a field on the right to a lane.

Cross the lane and take the path opposite (signed Romsley Hill) with a hedge on the left. As the hill (928 ft) is climbed there is a panoramic view to the left with Halesowen in the foreground and across to Birmingham City Centre on the far horizon. When a cream bungalow is reached on the left at the highest point of the hill bear slightly right to continue on the path with hawthorn bushes on the right.

The path shortly curves around the edge of a field towards houses and a radio mast on the left. (There are two masts in view at this point, but you ignore the one to the right.) Emerge on a road (Farley Lane) and turn right, passing to your left the triangular village green and, also on the left after about a further 200 yards, is Romsley Water Tower. At the next junction the lane bears left around a bend – after about 100 yards take a path on the left that is adjacent to a bungalow named 'Foxgloves'. Now follow this path (part of the North Worcestershire Path) by clear waymarks to the Manchester Inn on the main road (B4551).

From the inn turn right and take the left turn at the next junction which crosses the M5 and passes farm buildings. At a junction of tracks bear right to follow a track with high holly hedges for about half a mile, then turn left at a stile by the National Trust sign. Entering a wood swing right to pass a stream and two pools on the right and then follow a broad green way through gorse to the top of the ridge. This is a very picturesque path.

Turn half right along the ridge to the summit of Waseley Hill (1013 ft) marked by a conifer wood, then retrace your steps and walk north along the ridge (fence on left) to the summit of Windmill Hill (928 ft) which has a toposcope and good views of the Worcestershire countryside to the south and over South Birmingham to the north.

Descend to the Visitor Centre and turn left along Gannow Green Lane. Cross the M5 and turn right into Newtown Lane. After about 50 yards take the path on the left, keeping a hedge on the right for about 400 yards, then meeting a gate and stile on the right go left down to the bottom of the field. Cross a stile to the left of a tree followed immediately by another stile.

Follow the right-hand hedge in the next field to drop down to a stream and then bear right across a meadow to reach a gate and a stile in the top right corner. Cross the stile and proceed with a fence on the right and, at a wood, turn left for a few yards and then right to walk with the edge of the wood for approximately 180 yards. Turn right and take the wide track through Ell Wood (this is a permissive path only and not a right of way).

Ell Wood, and also Coopers Wood met later on this walk, are ancient woodlands which are small, surviving parts of the woods that once almost covered Britain after the last Ice Age, around 8,000 years ago. Ell Wood is best seen during the spring when parts of it are carpeted with bluebells.

This track curves gradually to the left and becomes narrower – keep on the main track ignoring side tracks. Emerging from the wood at a junction of tracks bear left along the track for about 100 yards and then turn right up a track, fenced on both sides, then hedged, to a lane.

Turn left along the lane and after about a quarter of a mile, where the road crosses a depression, turn left through gates leading to Brook House Farm. Follow the driveway round until it swings away to the right towards a large metal barn. Here go left along a path with woodland on the left and a small conifer plantation on the right.

Cross a stile and head for the far right-hand corner of the field. Then, in the next field, keep to the right-hand hedge around the field to a stile in the far corner.

Do not cross this stile but turn left and follow a waymarked path across two fields; and in a third field bear right with a hedge on the right to meet a track: go along this to very soon cross a stile. Now follow the path which swings left to Lower Illey Farm. Here turn right along a surfaced track, signed Illey, and continue along this to reach Illey.

The shorter walk ends here.

Remarkably Illey has retained its rural character in spite of being within the Borough of Dudley and so close to the conurbation.

Cross Illey Lane near the Black Horse pub and take a path opposite (signed Lapal and Woodgate) which is a wide track for approximately a quarter of a mile.

At the end of the track swing left to go over a stile and a footbridge left of Coopers Wood. Then go right to cross a stile and walk another farm track which twists and turns for half a mile to reach a junction of tracks about 100 yds after passing under power lines. Here turn right up the track to a lane (Lye Close Lane) which you follow, turning right over the motorway bridge and on to reach Carters Lane. Turn right for a few yards and then left into Clapgate Lane and back to Woodgate.

6

Chaddesley Corbett and an 'unnamed' hill

This walk starting from half-timbered Chaddesley Corbett, explores some comparatively remote countryside close to Bromsgrove. Passing through the 'away from it all' hamlets of Purshull Green, Cooksey Green and Rushock it rises to the humble height of an unnamed hill.

Distance: 12 miles or 8 miles
Maps: Landranger 139; Pathfinder 953/974
Car Parking: Roadsides in Chaddesley Corbett
Public Transport: Midland Red West 133/134
(Kidderminster-Bromsgrove)
Start/Finish: Chaddesley Corbett (GR892735)
Refreshments: Pub, Park Gate
Shortened Version: The walk can be shortened to 8 miles by turning right at Durrance Farm (GR911712) and taking the lane to Cooksey Green.

LEAVE Chaddesley Corbett by taking the path signed 'Chaddesley Woods' opposite the Swan Inn. Bear left beside a market garden along a wide track with a hedge on the left, soon becoming a path with a bank on the right. Cross a stile onto tarmac and continue on the same heading, the tarmac soon becoming a track. Continue forward through several fields to reach Chaddesley Woods.

On reaching Chaddesley Woods, a National Nature Reserve, climb the stile and go straight ahead. When this track meets a T-junction turn right, then at another T-junction turn right along the main track and go straight on to reach the main road (A448). Cross the road and take another path at the left of Outwood Farm.

Walk with a hedge on the right through two fields,, then in a third go diagonally left towards a pylon. At the pylon cross a stream and stile on the right and go forward with a hedge and fence on the right. Soon cross a stile on the right and continue with the hedge now on the left. Cross a

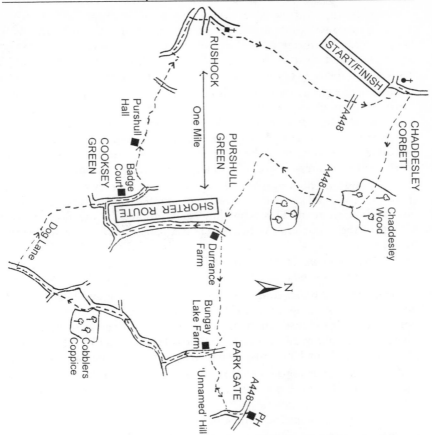

stile to the right of a house to emerge at Purshull Green. Go forward along a cinder track and soon veer left across open grassland and turn left just past a modern bungalow on your right. Cross the meadow, keeping the hedge on the right, and then go through two hunter's gates that are close together to enter the next field.

Ascend the slope and then descend in this large field to go under a pylon line and over a fence stile left of a pylon. Then walk with a hedge on the left through the next field, cross a stile and then descend straight across a meadow to cross a bridge over a brook, bear slightly left over a fence stile and ascend a field with an old orchard on the right to reach a lane (Berry Lane).

If you are taking the shorter route turn right here and take the lane to Cooksey Green. Here turn left and descend the lane to Badge Court. Then continue reading from ✳ on page 27.

Cross the lane and take a path through several metal gates and bear left across a meadow, going under pylon lines right of a pylon to follow a hedge on the left through two large fields. At a metal stile cross a hollow green track and go straight across the next field; then cross a footbridge just right of the field corner to bear left across the next two fields.

Now veer right across a third field to a lane (near Bungay Lake Farm). Turn right and almost immediately go left over a stile, across a field and over a footbridge. Walk with a hedge on the left to reach a fence stile: go over this and then bear right to climb a steep slope to the trig point (348 ft), not quite on the summit of the unnamed hill. There are good views of the surrounding countryside from here despite its modest height.

Trig points are no longer used by the Ordnance Survey but, because of their value to walkers, some have been adopted by walking groups to ensure their survival. This point has been adopted by the Bromsgrove Group of the Ramblers' Association and a plaque carries the following inscription:

To commemorate the Diamond Jubilee of the Ramblers' Association in 1995 this pillar was adopted by the Bromsgrove Group.

From the trig point continue forward on your original heading and down to a track along a short ridge. Go left along this and past a large house (Warridge House) on the right; go along its driveway to a lane and turn left. After about 250 yards the main road is reached (A448). Turn left along this for about 100 yards, then turn right to reach the Park Gate Inn.

At the time of writing a diversion order for the path near Warridge House was being sought. If this is successful you may find that the route is slightly different from that described in the previous paragraph. However, waymarks should make the route clear.

After refreshment, retrace your steps back past Warridge House, over the unnamed hill, down to the fence stile and along to recross the bridge, then back across the field to the lane near Bungay Lake Farm.

Turn left to pass the farm and continue for a quarter of a mile, then turn right at a junction and, ignoring a right fork just after going under power lines, follow the lane for one mile to the edge of Cobblers Coppice. Enter the coppice through a hunter's gate and take the bridleway on the right-hand edge of the coppice, then on the edge of a field, to reach a lane. Turn right and then immediately left at the T-junction of roads. After half a mile, just past Cooksey Corner Cottage, turn right down Dog Lane which soon becomes an attractive bridleway through the trees for about one mile to Cooksey Green (although it can be very muddy!).

When the bridleway reaches a lane turn right to the hamlet of Cooksey Green; then, passing a junction, descend the lane to Badge Court.

✷ *Continue from here if you are following the shorter walk.*

Pass Badge Court (fronted by an attractive pool) on the left. Continue on the lane for a further quarter of a mile and then, after passing a modern house on the left and a farm on the right, turn left along a surfaced drive leading to Purshull Hall.

This area, including both Badge Court and Purshull Hall, featured in the religious strife of the seventeenth century. Badge Court was built around 1630 of half timber and brick; Purshull Hall is of several periods and was a papist stronghold, with a secret chapel and priest's hide.

Entering the farmyard of Purshull Hall keep to the right boundary, past farm implements, to reach a stile to the right of a barn. Cross this and walk diagonally across a meadow and continue with a hedge on the right until a bridge over the brook is reached.

Cross the bridge and walk with a hedge on the left, crossing a stile after about 75 yards. Then, after another 100 yards go through a gate and turn right to walk with a hedge on the right for about 200 yards. After the hedge swings left (and ignoring an earlier stile) cross a footbridge and a stile. Bear left across a marshy field to a stile in the opposite hedge, cross the stile and a footbridge (it is usually very muddy here!) and walk through the rear garden of a cottage (this was formerly Rushock Post Office) to a lane.

Cross the lane and go through a gate and bear left across the field towards a white house where there is a stile to another lane. Turn right for about a quarter of a mile (good views of the Malverns to the left) and then take the path on the right just before reaching a black and white house ('Little Hyde'): go straight ahead with trees on the left and shortly, when the trees end, bear left to go over a metal gate (not waymarked) and then maintain the same heading across a field to a stile in the far boundary.

Cross the narrow lane and go over the stile opposite to bear slightly left to cross a meadow and emerge on a lane by the entrance to Court Farm. Go right along the lane to Rushock Church, passing the Old Rectory on the left.

From Rushock Church take the path that goes in a northerly direction, starting opposite a modern bungalow named 'Ridge House'. Shortly a stile is reached; cross this and bear slightly right to go briefly across a meadow and then along a tree lined track that soon slopes to the left to a stile. Turn right to walk along the field with a hedge on the right; go over another stile and walk straight across the large field. Then, on the same heading walk with a hedge on the left through the next field and go straight across the following field: at the end of this cross a wide grassed track (which is used for horse racing occasionally). Still on the same heading go straight across a large meadow at the end of which a farm track is crossed, before you cross the next field on the same heading to the main road (A448).

Cross the main road and turn left and in approximately 100 yards turn right on a path which is immediately right of a nursery (Rowberry's). Continue on the path with a ditch on the right, and curve around the field, keeping to the right-hand boundary: ignore the *first* stile on the right leading to a pool, but go over the *second* stile in the right-hand hedge and turn left along a track. (*The second stile is about 280 yards from the A448.*) After approximately 150 yards a T-junction of tracks is reached; here turn left to retrace your outward steps to Chaddesley Corbett.

7

Hanbury and Pipers Hill

Exploring the scattered village of Hanbury with its fine church situated on a memorable hilltop site with extensive views of the Worcestershire countryside this ramble also has good viewpoints from the climbs to Puck Hill and Pipers Hill and includes a scenic stretch of parkland at Hanbury Hall.

Distance: 11 miles
Maps: Landranger 150; Pathfinder 974
Car Parking: Roadsides in Hadzor (GR917618)
Public Transport (*adds 3¾ miles*): Buses and trains to Droitwich. From Droitwich walk east along the B4090 and, just after passing under the M5, go right along a lane to Hadzor.
Refreshments: Café – Jinney Ring Craft Centre; Pub – Hanbury Wharf
Place of Interest: Hanbury Hall (National Trust)

COMMENCE the walk at Hadzor, a hamlet of picturesque cottages set in generous gardens, going southwards along the lane until it bends sharply right; here turn left down a track which is a signed footpath. Go over a stile by a white cottage and go over further stiles through three fields, bearing right, through a kissing gate and left down a stony driveway of a large house. At the lane turn left over the canal bridge and shortly go over a second bridge, then turn immediately right on a track marked Brookhouse Farm.

After about 100 yds, where the track swings right, go across a meadow on the same heading and under a railway bridge (left of the far right corner of the field); continue on the same heading (SSE) through four fields (following the Wychavon Way signs), then, on the same heading, through the edge of a copse left of Dean Brook. The path then follows the boundary of the field with a hedge on the right round to a stile and waymark indicating the path at the edge of Puckhill Wood for about half a mile to a lane.

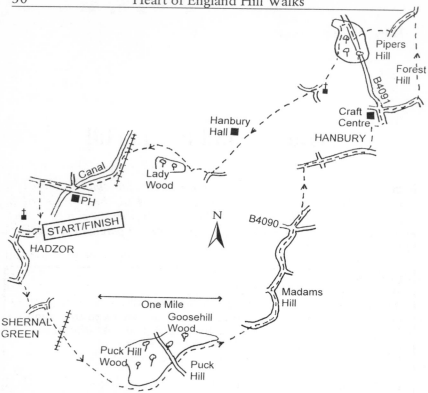

Cross the lane and bear left on a path through a field to Goosehill Wood and which then goes right along a track on the edge of the wood. At the end of the wood, at Puck Hill, go left over a stile and follow a waymarked path bearing right over two more stiles and past a caravan and through a copse of young trees.

At the end of the copse cross a horse jump to the left of a stile and go diagonally across the field towards a modern house. Go through a gate to the left of the house and then turn left along the drive for a few yards. Turn right at a track which twists and turns for half a mile, passing Madams Hill on the right.

When the track ends at a lane turn left and in half a mile cross the main road (B4090) and continue up the lane opposite for about 200 yards and just after passing under electricity lines and before the road bends right, cross a signposted stile on the left. Now take the path which goes half right (north) across two fields and out onto a lane by a black and white cottage: here turn right.

Proceed along the lane for approximately half a mile and, just past a house on the right called 'Appleby' take a path on the left to bear right across the field to a stile in the top right-hand corner. Continue with a hedge on the right and then through a copse of young trees for about 50 yards before turning right over a bridge stile and across a field and down a passageway between houses to a road (B4091).

At the road turn left and after about 200 yards turn right into Forest Lane (opposite Jinney Ring Craft Centre) and after about a quarter of a mile (where the road bends right) take a signed bridleway, which is an attractive tree-lined route to the left of the Forest Hill ridge.

When a lane is reached turn left for about 300 yds and then, where the lane turns left, take a path on the right (between cottages) through an old orchard with a hedge on the right and then through a field with a fence on the left to the farm on the left. Then climb straight up Pipers Hill (388 ft) to the left of the concrete drive; there are excellent views northwards to the Clent and Lickey Hills from here.

Now cross a cattle grid and go straight on (S W) through the woodland (Pipers Hill Common) to the road (B4091) and turn right. After 150 yards turn left on a track at the edge of a wood by a parking area and soon pass a pool on the left. After about 200 yards reach Knotts Farm where the track becomes a path which continues along the the western edge of the woodland for about half a mile where a junction of tracks is reached by a large oak tree.

The avenue of oaks leading to Hanbury Hall

Here continue forward on the same heading on the path which climbs to Hanbury's hilltop church (329 ft).

Hanbury Parish Church, dedicated to St Mary the Virgin, is built of the local Bromsgrove sandstone and its memorable hilltop site may possibly have been a fort in Roman times. In Saxon times, in AD836, there was a monastery here.

After admiring the extensive views which include Madams Hill in the near distance, to the Malverns and Bredon on the horizon, turn down the steep lane in front of the church and after a few yards take a path at the junction of lanes which goes through a kissing gate by a National Trust sign. The path which goes straight ahead through the large meadow and then along an avenue of mature oak trees has lovely views to the Malverns to the right.

Where the avenue bears slightly to the right, bear left of a small wire fence enclosure containing young trees. Cross the tarmac drive and continue on the same heading past two pools on your right aiming to go in front (left) of Hanbury Hall, noting the ha-ha as you approach the Hall. Cross a stile and go forward in front of the Hall.

This impressive house was built in 1701 for the Vernon family and is now owned by the National Trust, being open to the public at advertised times.

Past the Hall keep on the same straight heading across the parkland (initially with the ha-ha on the right, then straight forward as the ha-ha curves away right) and emerge by a stile left of a small pool at a bend in the lane. Here turn immediately right over a stile and walk with a fence and the pool on the right for a few yards and then bear left, still with a fence on the right. Cross a stile and go round the edge of a field with a hedge on the right, then cross a bridge stile and go up a meadow (300 degrees) passing Lady Wood over to the left.

Pass a small pool on the right, then leave the meadow by a gate and bear left to go diagonally across a sloping open meadow for about 100 yards to cross a farm track and then go right through a hunter's gate. Continue forward with a hedge on the right to shortly cross a railway bridge and then down a short track bordered by hawthorn trees to reach a bridge over the Worcester and Birmingham Canal. Do not cross the bridge but go slightly left, then over a stile onto the towpath.

Turn left along the canal and leave the towpath at Hanbury Wharf (bridge 35). Turn right along the road (B4090) for approximately 400 yards. Turn left on a farm track (signed Wychavon Way) and soon pass Home Farm on the right; then continue with a wood (Ash Coppice) on the right to a T-junction of tracks where you turn right. At farm buildings bear right to go over a stile on the left and in a few yards another stile to a lane. Turn left to Hadzor and the end of the walk.

8

Elmley Castle and Bredon Hill

Bredon Hill is a high plateau above the Vale of Evesham surrounded by a string of splendid villages. The walk commences at Elmley Castle which has a wide main street with houses mainly of timber framed architecture and is one of Worcestershire's most appealing villages.

Distance: 12 miles or 9½ miles
Maps: Landranger 150; Pathfinder 1019/1042
Car Parking: Elmley Castle (roadside)
Start/Finish: Elmley Castle (GR983412)
Refreshments: Pubs, Conderton and Ashton-under-Hill; Café, Conderton
Shortened version: The walk can easily be shortened to 9½ miles by returning to Elmley Castle direct from Kemerton

---

FROM Elmley Castle main street turn right at the Queen Elizabeth Inn along Mill Lane which, after almost half a mile turns to the left and steadily climbs, becoming a bridleway at Hill House Farm. Continue along the bridleway and just past a gate go half left and climb a track towards trees on the horizon.

Go through a gate and along a rough track ignoring a bridleway to the left and soon, when a wood on the left is reached, bear right up a steep green track, almost to the top of the ridge; and when a wire fence is met turn right along a broad green track, which soon passes a small wood on the left, for about half a mile to the 'tower'.

This fine path follows the ridge which is the highest part of Bredon Hill at 961 ft and from here there are extensive and unforgettable views to the Combertons, the Avon Valley and well beyond. The 'tower' is reputed to have been built by a Mr Parsons of Kemerton during the eighteenth century as a folly.

From the tower continue on the same heading with a wall on the right and through a small wood. Out of the wood turn sharply right and go through a gate almost hidden in the trees. Bear right along a rough green

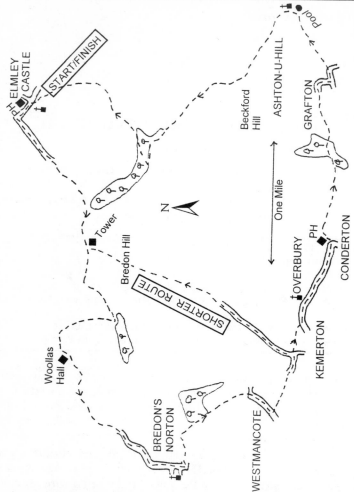

track through a bumpy field with hawthorn bushes, descending to two metal gates. Go through the left gate and bear right to descend a steep meadow to a new stile in the far right corner of this meadow.

Turn left down a farm track and shortly, at the next metal gate, bear left across a meadow, crossing a stream just right of Woollas Hall. Over the stile turn left along the drive and walk in between buildings and out onto a bridleway, which becomes a lane, for approximately 1½ miles to Bredons Norton.

Ignore a right turn at Home Farm and then, very shortly, and still on the same heading go along the lane, which is also a public footpath (signed

Bredon Hill 1). The lane soon bends to the left past a house on the left and in a few yards goes through a gate, then bears to the right up a meadow to another gate. Go through this gate and straight up a second meadow until level with a house on the left.

At this point turn right and follow a path bearing slightly left across a field, then, with a wood on the left go through a second field and, with a hedge on the right through two more fields. Then bear right on a track to take a lane to Westmancote where, opposite a wall post-box, turn left along a path through two fields to Kemerton. When the path emerges in a residential road cross over and take a lane on the same heading for about 150 yards to a house called Kings Lea.

If you are walking the shortened version this is where you branch off. For the longer walk continue reading from ✱ on page 36.

From Kings Lea turn left to climb the lane out of Kemerton which eventually passes Bells Castle on the left, and climbs steeply to end at a metal gate close to a barn on the right. Go through the metal gate and straight ahead along an unfenced track: soon bear slightly right off the track to take a path through a wood.

When you emerge from the wood the bridleway continues with a wood

On Bredon Hill. The Banbury Stone

and a wall on the right. Past the wood the clear wide track climbs, still with a wall on the right, and open views all round. Keep straight ahead, ignoring side tracks, until eventually the path meets the ridge. From here turn right to retrace your earlier steps back to Elmley Castle.

✳   Opposite this house go through a gate and through a large field, then veer right to cross a small meadow to a road and turn left. Proceed along the road via Overbury to Conderton.

Overbury is a stone built village of substantial, mainly Georgian, architecture. The much restored church has some interesting features including a Norman nave and an Early English chancel. Overbury Court is an eighteenth century building with a garden and parkland containing some rare trees.

In Conderton at the Yew Tree Inn turn left up a lane for 120 yards and then take a path on the right beside a stone wall and walk with a hedge/fence of the right for four fields, crossing a track after the third field. Then swing left up a slope on a green track and then through a wooden gate. Veering slightly to the right carry on up a meadow and through another gate through a narrow belt of trees, emerging onto a ridge.

Swing right to go over a stile in a wire fence and cross two fields, going right of large willow trees to reach Grafton. Walk through the village until a T-junction at Middle Farm is reached: here turn left and, where the lane bends to the right, continue straight on a path across a meadow, over a stream, and continue with a hedge on the left until a track is reached. After passing a large house on the left go left across a meadow to a metal gate in the far corner and past a pool on the right to Aston-under-Hill church. This is a very picturesque spot.

From the churchyard go straight up the hill (Beckford Hill – part of the Bredon plateau) to the left following the Wychavon Way waymarks (which you will now follow until almost the end of this walk). From here there are good views south to Dumbleton Hill.

When a track is reached go straight over, continuing up the steep hill. Soon the ground flattens: continue on the same heading (310 degrees) soon to climb again, still following the Wychavon Way signs, until the ridge is reached. At this point turn right for a few yards and then go left, firstly with a stone wall on the right, then with a wire fence for three quarters of a mile.

The path now continues on the same heading but with a wood on the right until a cross-roads of tracks is met: here turn right and descend a bridleway through woodlands and then along a track, across a sloping, marshy meadow and through a copse. At a junction of paths (where you now leave the Wychavon Way) go through a metal gate, cross a stream, turn right and take the path bearing slightly to the left (passing a large oak tree on your left) to cross a large meadow and cross a stile in its far boundary.

Turn left and walk with a hedge/fence on the left around a field until you meet a stile on the left. Cross a small meadow, then bear right on a path with a pool on the left to emerge in Elmley Castle churchyard and back to your starting point.

9

The Malverns

This walk features the magnificent ridge of hills that once divided the former separate shires of Hereford and Worcester. There are superb views, to the west, of the Herefordshire countryside and away to Wales; and, to the east, the elegant spa town of Great Malvern flanked by the smaller settlements of Malvern Link and Malvern Wells, with the wide expanse of the Severn plain beyond.

Distance: 12 miles or 9 miles
Maps: Landranger 150; Pathfinder 1018
Car Parking: Car park at British Camp
Public Transport: Train to Colwall (Birmingham to Hereford line). Start reading from page 39.
Start/Finish: Malvern Hills Hotel (GR764403)
Refreshments: Pubs, Colwall Stone and Mathon; Café, Upper Colwall
Shortened Version: The walk can be shortened to 9 miles by starting/finishing at Colwall Station (GR757425) and using the road (B4218) between Wyche Cutting and Colwall Stone. Start reading from page 39.

FROM the Malvern Hills Hotel at British Camp cross the road (B4232) and take a path, signed Worcestershire Way, immediately left of a toilet block. Follow this path over stiles through four fields and then right along a green track. Continue following the Worcestershire Way waymarks to reach a lane.

Turn left along the lane for a quarter of a mile and then go right, by some attractive black and white cottages, along a track for a few yards; this soon becomes a path with a fence on the left for approximately 300 yards. Now bear left across a field, then walk with a hedge on the right for about 100 yards before turning right over the second stile to go through two fields and to cross a railway bridge to reach Colwall Stone.

Start here if you are travelling by train or doing the shorter walk.

Turn right at the Post Office on the B4218 for about a quarter of a mile, then take a left fork (Brockhill Road). Just past The Downs School music block turn left on a path past a small lake on the right, then bear left through a small copse and across two fields to a white house. Turn right along the lane for approximately half a mile.

At the next junction turn left (signed Mathon) and after a quarter of a mile reach another junction; here take a path (signed Mathon Court) and walk with a hedge on the left and later a pool on the left. Reaching a cricket pitch cut across the edge of it to the gateway of Mathon Court, which has

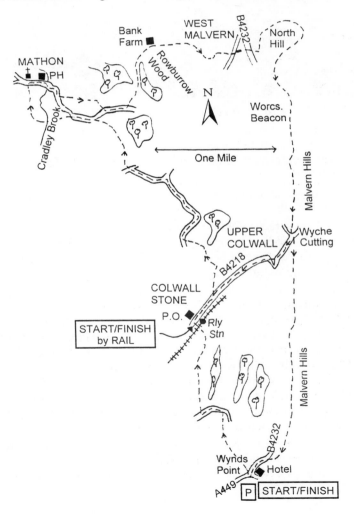

One of the stone direction markers on the Malvern Hills

an impressive avenue of mature horse chestnut trees. At the lane turn right (signed Mathon, Cradley) for about 250 yards and then left along a sandy track to Warners Farm, then on a path to the right of the farm buildings to Cradley Brook.

Cross the brook and turn right to cross two stiles; then, at a junction of tracks, turn right along a green track to Mathon.

Mathon is an attractive cluster of cottages, mainly black and white, in what used to be a significant hop growing area. It has a fine church built by the monks of Pershore Abbey, and the churchyard contains a yew tree reputed to be a thousand years old.

Turn right at Mathon church, cross Cradley Brook again, and in a quarter of a mile turn left on a path which goes with another brook on the right to cross three fields to reach a track. Turn right to a lane, turn left along this and after about 150 yds turn left on a path that bears right of farm buildings and climbs a slope to go through the edge of Rowberrow Wood. The path then climbs steeply between woods, then bears right to pass the end of Rowberrow Wood and to reach farm buildings (Bank Farm). Here bear right and descend a lane to a stream. The lane then climbs through trees and, at a right-hand bend, leave the lane and take a path on the left (signed Worcestershire Way).

The path veers right to climb a steep bank: on the top go over a stile to the left of pine trees and go straight ahead and through a farmyard (this can be very muddy). Now take the same heading on a residential road to a T-junction. Turn left up a steep road (Croft Bank) to a cross-roads at West Malvern.

Go straight over and take the steep lane for a few yards, then go left along a wide path passing to the left of a metal weather-vane. Keep on the main path which bears right around the hill and climb to the summit of North Hill (1293 ft). Then descend and make for the main track leading to the Worcestershire Beacon. This is the highest point of the range at 1395 ft and there are almost unlimited views from the toposcope.

These are some of Housman's 'blue remembered hills' and the hills that inspired the music of Worcestershire-born Sir Edward Elgar whose birthplace, a cottage at Lower Broadheath a few miles from here, is now a museum open to the public at advertised times.

Now proceed southwards on the ridge track which provides a fine walk for three miles back to British Camp, via Wyche Cutting (where you cross the road and then ascend by steps beside a shelter and toilets).

If you are doing the shorter walk return to Colwall Stone and the railway station from Wyche Cutting by turning left along the road (B4218).

For the complete walk ending at the railway station now follow the instructions in the first two paragraphs.

The summit of the Worcestershire Beacon

10

Bosbury and Oyster Hill

The walk commences at Ledbury, an attractive country market town with many black and white buildings of character, including the Market House dating from around 1650. The village of Bosbury also has good black and white architecture in its wide main street, and Oyster Hill rises from this exquisite countryside west of the Malverns which is famed for its fruit and hops.

Distance: 10½ miles
Maps: Landranger 149; Pathfinder 1018/1041
Car Parking: Public car park, Bye Street, Ledbury
Public Transport: Trains to Ledbury (Birmingham – Hereford line)
Start/Finish: Ledbury (GR710377)
Refreshments: Pubs, Bosbury; Cafés, Ledbury

L EAVE Ledbury via Church Lane, a cobbled street of black and white houses that is one of the most photographed streets in Britain. Bear left at the Magistrates House along Church Road and at the next junction go right up the hill, and where the lane bears left go straight on along a path (signed Dog Hill Wood). The path has housing to the left and woodland to the right.

After a quarter of a mile cross a lane (Knapp Lane) and take a track which winds around to Frith Wood House. Immediately before the gate to the house turn left and take the path with a hedge on the right, passing Frith Wood House. Go through a field followed by a cottage garden, then bear right through orchards. Keep straight ahead with Frith Wood on the right and then on the same heading past a converted oast-house to reach Frith Farm.

Here take a signed path on the right following waymarks along the edge of woodland for half a mile. Take a waymarked path (*LR19*) left with a hedge on the right down a sloping field for about 200 yards, then turn right through a gate (*LR20*) bearing left across a large field to walk with a hedge on the right through the next field. At a solitary oak tree bear left

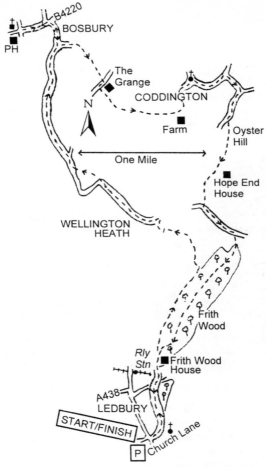

through a gate and over a stile: the path continues at the left-hand side of a young woodland plantation and then climbs steeply with a hedge on the left. There are good views of surrounding hills from here.

Just over the brow of the hill go left over a stile in the corner of the field and along a track for a few yards to turn right on a narrow lane (Ochre Hill) and, shortly at a T-junction, turn right up the wide lane.

At the next junction turn left on the road that skirts the village of Wellington Heath and go straight on, passing the parish church on the left for approximately three quarters of a mile. Where the road bends sharply to the left go right on a path across a field and gradually bear slightly left to emerge on the road well left of a stream (GR702415). At the road turn right. Reaching a fork take the left-hand lane for just over a mile to the B4220 at Bosbury, and turn left to walk through the village.

Bosbury has a main street with attractive timber framed houses and an inn. Opposite is Holy Trinity Church, a large building built mainly around 1180, the transitional period in church architecture between Norman and Early English. The detached bell tower, a feature of some Herefordshire churches, was probably built at a later date.

Bosbury Church with its detached bell tower

Retrace your steps along the B4220 and turn right the lane (that you previously walked) for about a quarter of a mile, then turn left along a track. When gates are reached at the end of the track go diagonally right, on a bridleway that is not signposted (*Bosbury No. 73*), across a field and over a fence (no stile) and continue on the same heading through the next field to emerge immediately right of farm buildings on the lane.

Turn right and immediately past 'The Grange' take a path on the left, soon with a hop-yard on the left, to cross a stream, then go on the same heading through the next field. In the following field bear left to walk with a hedge on the left to a narrow lane just north of Woofields Farm. Turn left, and shortly take a path on the left, through a garden, left of a pool and then bear left through an orchard on a slope.

Go over a stile to walk with a hedge on the right, then go right through a metal gate along a track and shortly, at a T-junction, turn left on a lane. Turn right at Coddington Church and stay on this lane for approximately half a mile, then turn right at a T-junction (signed Wellington Heath) and, after a quarter of a mile, turn right again up a steep lane.

Where the lane bends to the right and starts to descend take the track on the left through the trees which climbs to the summit of Oyster Hill (685 ft). From the summit there are extensive views over the Herefordshire countryside and of the Malvern Hills.

From here descend on the path with Berrington Woods on the right and a field on the left, then on the same heading through the spacious parkland of Hope End House with its many mature oak trees to descend the slope to a lane at Hope End Farm.

Hope End House was once the home of author Elizabeth Barratt Browning where she spent a happy childhood among these hills.

Turn left along the lane for approximately half a mile, then cross a stile on the right and take a path (CW57) bearing right across a meadow to ascend the slope into Frith Wood. Continue on this ridge path through the trees which eventually descends steeply to a T-junction of tracks (after approximately 1¼ miles); turn right and follow the path to a wide forestry track and turn left: the path soon passes through the garden of Frith Wood House. From here you retrace your outward steps, crossing Knapp Lane and taking the path at the edge of Dog Hill Wood back to Ledbury town centre.

Ledbury, Church Lane

11

Henley-in-Arden and The Mount

This walk starts from the small Warwickshire town of Henley-in-Arden where many of the sixteenth century timber framed houses in the long and distinctive High Street are built of oak from the ancient Forest of Arden. It has a fifteenth century Guildhall and the remains of a medieval market cross. The walk reaches the lowly height of The Mount, explores the attractive villages of Aston Cantlow and Wootton Wawen, and goes via the Rough Hills and the Stratford-upon-Avon Canal.

Distance: 13 miles or 6½ miles
Maps: Landranger 151; Pathfinder 975
Car Parking: Street sides in Henley-in-Arden
Public Transport: Bus: Stratford Blue X20 (Birmingham – Stratford-upon-Avon); Train: Birmingham Snow Hill – Stratford-upon-Avon. Alight at Henley-in-Arden
Start/Finish: Henley-in-Arden (GR151662)
Refreshments: Pubs in Henley, Aston Cantlow and Wootton Wawen. Cafés in Henley
Shortened Version: This walk can be shortened to 6½ miles by returning to Henley from Wootton Wawen, thus eliminating the southern section of the route.

L EAVE the main street (A3400) at Henley Parish Church and walk down Beaudesert Lane, soon passing on the left the eleventh century Beaudesert Parish Church of St Nicholas with its impressive Norman doorway, and go through a kissing gate to climb to the modest summit of The Mount with its views over the rooftops of Henley and the adjoining parish of Beaudesert. The Mount was the site of an eleventh century fortified Norman castle of wood and stone built by Thurston de Montfort.

Follow the main track over the crest of the hill into a dip and up again to take a path on the right (stile in right-hand corner of the field). Bear slightly left across the meadow to a stile to a lane and turn left; after

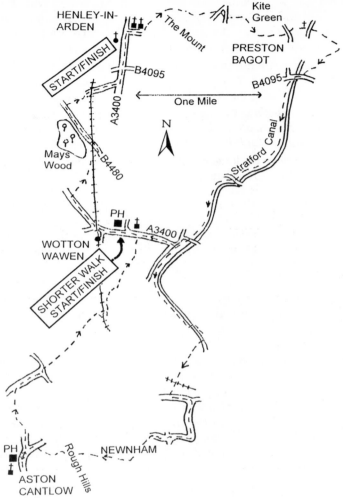

approximately a quarter of a mile go through a gate to take a path on the right near a cream cottage (Kates Cottage). Keep to the left-hand hedge to reach a stile in the left corner of the field, turn left and immediately cross another stile to go straight across a field to a stile opposite. Carry on the same heading across three more fields to emerge on a lane. Cross over and go through a kissing gate to take the steep path to Preston Bagot Church.

This church stands on a modest hilltop site with lovely views of the surrounding countryside. Cross the lane and take a path opposite the church gate across a meadow and through a gateway. Walk through this long field and cross a stile and footbridge in the left-hand corner, over a brook. Turn right up the slope to cross the canal bridge and turn right onto the towpath of the Stratford-upon-Avon Canal.

Walk the left-hand canal towpath for half a mile until bridge no. 48 is reached, then cross to the right-hand towpath and continue for a further 2½ miles, crossing the A3400 by a fine iron aqueduct.

If you are walking the shorter version, leave the canal at this aqueduct and turn left to walk a short distance along the main road (A3400) to Wootton Wawen and then continue from ✳ on page 49.

Continuing on the longer walk cross to the left-hand side again at bridge 55, about 300 yards before leaving the canal at bridge 56. Cross the bridge and in a few yards take a path on the left, adjacent to the entrance to Sillesbourne Rise. Keep to the right-hand hedge for some 200 yards and go right through a hedge stile and now follow the left-hand hedge to keep the same heading along a short track and over another stile. Follow the same heading and cross two further stiles to a railway line.

Cross the line with great care and go straight across the next field; cross a footbridge, and bear left to a stile under trees; then go straight across the field to a lane. Turn left and then right at the next junction, signed Newnham. At the Y-junction in Newnham turn left: after about 300 yards the road becomes a track and bends to the left; then after a quarter of a mile bends to the right (about 100 yds after the fence on the left ends).

When the track ends keep on the same heading with a hedge on the right, then bearing left to take a track down a slope through Rough Hill Wood. Then bear right and follow the right-hand hedge through the next field, then through an opening into another field, keeping to the right-hand fence, to reach the road. Turn left to explore the village of Aston Cantlow, which was once owned by the medieval de Cantilupe family. The church is reputed to be the wedding place of Shakespeare's parents.

Retrace your steps through the village and turn left at Chapel Lane and then take the path over the stile at the end of the lane and, after a few yards, cross a disused railway line. Go straight across a field to cross a footbridge and turn right to walk alongside the River Alne for a quarter of a mile, then strike off left across the field to a lane.

At the lane turn right into Little Alne and at the T-junction turn left, then almost immediately turn right over a stile and walk up the field (fence on left). Keep on the same heading and cross two more fields to a track. Cross the track and take a path on the right to a brick barn, then walk along the river to a lane.

Turn right along the lane and go under a railway bridge. In a few yards take a path on the left along a concrete drive and then bear right across the meadow to walk between the river and a sewage works, then subsequently along the river only, for half a mile before the path swings left to Wootton Wawen and emerges on the A3400 opposite the church.

The name Wootton Wawen is derived from a 'Saxon farm by the wood' and was founded in AD723. The prominently situated and imposing parish church dedicated to St Peter is believed to be the oldest church building in Warwickshire and is built on the site of an even earlier church. It contains Anglo-Saxon and Norman features dating from the twelfth to the fifteenth centuries. Nearby Wootton Hall, beyond the waterfall on the River Alne, is an Italian style late seventeenth century mansion. It is such a pity that this most attractive village is bisected by the thunderous roar of the A3400.

✳ *Continue from here on the shorter route.*

Turn left and left again into Alcester Road (B4089) and after a quarter of a mile pass under a railway bridge at Wootton Wawen station; then immediately turn right into Gorse Lane. After half a mile, just past Gorse Cottage and a wooden stable, take the path on the right through a metal gate straight across a field, across a ditch and then, keeping a hedge on the left, to the next stile.

Go diagonally right across a field, then a railway cutting (*take care*), to emerge on a lane. Turn left and walk along the lane (B4080) for half a mile to then take a path on the right, just before reaching May Hill Farm. Go straight across the field with a line of trees on the left, then cross a small field to a telephone box and down the drive to the main road (A3400) and back to Henley.

12

The Shakespeare Villages and Oversley Hill

This walk, starting at 'Drunken' Bidford, explores 'Hungry' Grafton, 'Dodging' Exhall, 'Papist' Wixford and 'Beggarly' Broom – which are most of the villages in the doggerel supposed to have been composed by the famous bard when he had had too much to drink! It also includes a pleasant stretch of the River Avon and attains the modest height of Oversley Hill.

Distance: 13 miles or 10 miles
Maps: Landranger 150/151; Pathfinder 997
Car Parking: Car park at Bidford Bridge
Public Transport: Midland Red West 146 (Birmingham-Evesham via Bidford)
Start/Finish: Bidford-on-Avon (GR099517)
Refreshments: Pubs at Bidford, Welford, Temple Grafton and Barton; Café at Bidford
Shortened Version: The walk can be shortened to 10 miles by taking the lane direct from Ardens Grafton back to Bidford

---

FROM Bidford Bridge, take a path left from the B4085 (following the Heart of England Way waymarks) to bear right in the first field and continue through two more fields and a short track to Barton Weir. Turn right along a track for a few yards to the Cottage of Content Inn and turn left to walk along the road for three quarters of a mile; then turn left following a path to and along the right bank of the River Avon for two miles.

Eventually, when the Mill Fields caravan site is reached, walk through the small site, turn left down a lane for a few yards and then right at Mill House along a short path to a lane to Welford. Welford-on-Avon is a chocolate box village of thatched cottages with lovely gardens. Continue on the lane passing the parish church and turn left just before the junction with High Street, down a drive by Glebe Cottage and past Daffodil Cottage.

At the end of the drive continue on a path which passes Applegarth House and along a meadow with a hedge and gardens on the right until it

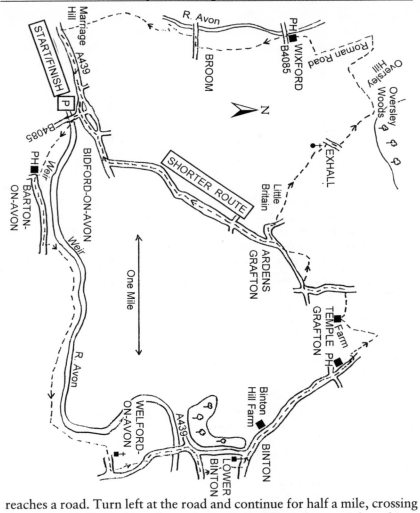

reaches a road. Turn left at the road and continue for half a mile, crossing the Avon, until reaching the main road (A439) and turn right: after a quarter of a mile take a path on the left straight across a meadow to a lane and turn left to Binton (not mentioned in the doggerel!).

Binton Parish Church, which was built in 1875, has blue lias walls with dressings of Cotswold stone. It has an interesting stained glass west window in memory of Sir Robert Falcon Scott, the famous explorer (Scott of the Antarctic), who stayed with his relatives at Binton Vicarage before his final ill-fated expedition in 1912.

From the church turn right and walk through the village, passing Binton

Hill Farm on the left, with the slope of Binton Hill behind it, for one mile until the crossroads and the Blue Boar Inn are reached. From the inn continue straight on the lane for a further quarter of a mile, then just past Barlwych House on the right turn left on a grassy track along a ridge to cross two meadows.

At a solitary ash tree turn left to follow a path with a hedge on the left. At the foot of the slope turn right to walk with a hedge on the right, and shortly over a stile in the corner of the field, to walk along a drive to the right of a house. (Although this path goes through a private garden it is a waymarked right of way.) At the gateway turn right and after a few yards turn left to walk with a hedge on the left through two meadows to a lane.

Turn left to Temple Grafton. In 1179 the manor of Temple Grafton was granted to Henry de Grafton. Later it passed to the Knights Templar who were responsible for building the original church. Hence the name 'Temple Grafton'. In Shakespeare's time poor soils in the area could have produced a low crop yield – hence the reference to 'Hungry Grafton'.

At the crossroads by the school turn right; then almost immediately turn right again on a path with gardens on the left to a hedge on the horizon. Turn left to walk with a hedge on the left around the field to the lane at Ardens Grafton. Turn right along this.

For the shorter walk turn left at the fork to return to Bidford-on-Avon.

Ardens Grafton has an attractive street of cottages, mainly built of local lias stone, which huddle snugly together on the ridge.

Continue on the lane for a quarter of a mile, then turn right down a steep lane to Little Britain.

At a junction by Orchard Farm cross a stile on the left and take a path on the left-hand side of a cottage, then go right of some sheds. Bear right across a meadow (keeping left of a telegraph post) to go right over a hidden stile. Bear left to the next stile in the hedge. Then walk with a hedge on the right for a few yards to cross a double stile and keep on the same heading with a hedge on the left through five fields to Exhall, probably known as 'Dodging Exhall' because of its comparative isolation prior to the eighteenth century.

At a lane turn right and soon turn left by Exhall Parish Notice Board to go across the cricket pitch and ascend Oversley Hill (340 ft). From its modest ridge there is a good view of peaceful Exhall and the Graftons beyond.

From a stile on the ridge go right, then almost immediately left over another stile, then straight on with a hedge on the right to descend to the corner of Oversley Wood. Turn left along a tree lined track for half a mile (ignoring a waymarked track on the right after about a quarter of a mile) and then right at a junction of tracks for a further half a mile, then left at a crossroads of tracks. (There is a view of Ragley Hall to the west from here.) This track (part of the Roman Road, Icknield Street) continues to Wixford Church where you turn right on a path past cottages.

'Papist' Wixford may be so-called because of its connections with the Throckmorton family of Coughton Court.

Ignoring the first waymarked path on the left, turn left through a meadow and a caravan park to the Fish Inn. Cross the road (B4085) and take the path (following the Heart of England Way waymarks) to the left of the river and then over a footbridge and a 'bumpy' meadow. Continue with a fence on the right through six fields and across a track, then retain the same heading through two fields, now with a hedge/fence on the left.

Bear right across a third field and via a metal gate and short drive to a lane at Broom ('Beggarly' Broom). Turn right, passing Broom Mills, and at a junction carry straight on along a track for about a quarter of a mile when it bears left to pass two thatched houses. Opposite the second thatched house go right across a meadow and a disused railway line to bear slightly right across a large field. Go across two meadows and, on the same heading, along a green track on the ridge of Marriage Hill. The track emerges on the main road (A439) where you turn left to return to Bidford.

The other places mentioned in the doggerel, although not visited on this walk, are 'Haunted' Hillborough, 'Piping' Pebworth and 'Dancing' Marston.

Bridge over the Avon at Bidford

13

The Tysoes and Edge Hill

The Tysoes, consisting of Upper, Middle and Lower Tysoe, are villages in South Warwickshire whose names are derived from Tiw, the heathen god of war. The walk also includes the escarpment of Edge Hill and a rewarding climb to Windmill Hill.

Distance: 12 miles or 10 miles
Maps: Landranger 151; Pathfinder 1021
Car Parking: Roadsides in Ratley
Start/Finish: Ratley (GR383473)
Refreshments: Pubs in Ratley, Middle Tysoe and Hornton; café and shops in Middle Tysoe
Shortened Version: The walk can easily be shortened to 10 miles by eliminating the climb to Windmill Hill.

! A brook to be crossed near the end of the walk may prove diffi-cult after prolonged rain.

RATLEY is a very peaceful cul-de-sac village built on a south facing slope in brown ironstone country and has an ancient parish church dating from 1250.

Starting from the triangular village green at Ratley Parish Church, walk west up the hill (via Church Street and High Street) to a T-junction on Edge Hill. Here take the path (following Centenary Way signs) which descends via steps through a wood, then goes left along a wide track at the foot of woodland; and where the track divides take the left fork up to the Castle Inn.

The Castle Inn occupies Edge Hill Tower, which is reputed to have been originally built as a place for 'entertaining' by Sanderson Miller of Radway. It resembles Guy's Tower at Warwick Castle.

From the inn turn sharp right, firstly on a concrete path and then on a soil path that meanders through the woods (still following the Centenary

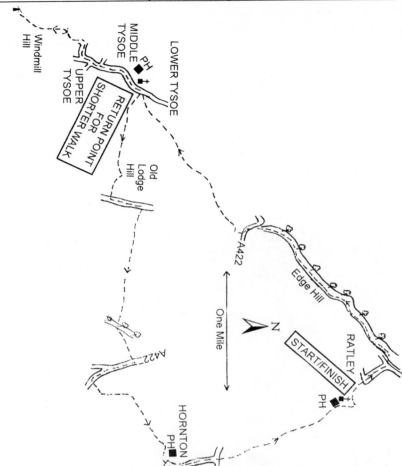

Way signs). Where the path divides, shortly before reaching a main road*,
fork right, soon with a field and fence on your left, until the path meets a
lane at Edge Hill Farm. Turn right immediately before the farm on a path
(still the Centenary Way), now running near the left-hand edge of the
woodland, until it reaches the main road (A422).

* *If you find yourself on this road, which runs from the A422 along Edge
Hill, you have come too far. Go back for about fifty yards looking for
the path at the fork. At the time of writing there was no Centenary Way
sign here.*

Cross the A422 (with great care!) and follow a track opposite and after about a hundred yards turn right along a track with farm buildings on the right, then shortly go left along a grassy track which soon leads to the grassy escarpment.

There are fine views from Edge Hill across the Warwickshire Feldon. The first major battle of the Civil War, the Battle of Edge Hill (1642), took place in the low-lying fields between Radway and Kineton.

Continue on the heading, soon with woods on the right, for a quarter of a mile, then follow a waymark, turning right down a slope through the wood. Emerge from the wood and bear diagonally right across the field (noting the ridge and furrow) to a gate in the far left corner.

Bear left in the next field and go over a stile, retaining the same heading to a gap in the far corner. Then walk straight along through two fields with a hedge on the right; and in the next field cut across diagonally

The restored windmill on Windmill Hill

bearing right to a stile and gate in the far right corner. Turn left on the lane to Middle Tysoe passing the impressive eleventh century church and many attractive cottages and the Peacock Inn in the main street.

If you are taking the shorter option return to Middle Tysoe church and then continue reading from ✪ below.

Go straight through the village to the adjoining settlement of Upper Tysoe. Here turn right at Shipston Road and, after a quarter of a mile, turn left into Smarts Lane* *(see below).* Where the lane ends go through a gate and turn right and across a field to a stile opposite and then turn left to walk with a hedge on the left up a very large field to the summit of Windmill Hill with its restored windmill.

This is a lovely bracing spot with magnificent views all round, including the Tysoes and Edge Hill to the north, and the great house of Compton Wynyates to the south. This evocative mellow Tudor building of the fifteenth and sixteenth centuries occupies a splendid site in between the hills, and has a garden containing sculptured yews.

After admiring the panorama from the top of the hill retrace your outward steps to Middle Tysoe church.

✪   *Rejoin the walk here if you have omitted Windmill Hill.*

After about 250 yards past the church take a bridleway on the right (this is through a gate to the right of the stile and gate used earlier in the walk) and go straight along the fenced track for just over half a mile when the track climbs up Old Lodge Hill at the left-hand edge of woodland. At the top of the hill and out of the wood turn left along a track for a quarter of a mile to the road and turn left. *The precise status of the track from the wood to the road is somewhat uncertain but it is well used and does appear to be a public bridleway.*

After almost a quarter of a mile turn right along a track, fenced on both sides, and when two metal gates close together are reached maintain the same heading across three fields, with a fence on the right; then, in a fourth bear left to walk near the edge of woodland. Then go straight across a large field (bearing 115 deg) to a narrow strip of woodland on the far side. Climb through the trees on a path beside a large oak on the right (rather

---

*   *The route described at this point does not strictly follow the right of way as shown on the OS map. This is reached by continuing along Shipston Road to a point on the left, shortly after the road turns right. However, at the time of writing, this right of way was impassable. The route via Smarts Lane is well used and is, apparently, the preferred way.*

overgrown at the time of writing) and go over a stile at the top of the ridge and across a field to the A422.

Turn right (take care – fast traffic!) for half a mile and then turn left on the drive to Hornton Grounds Quarry: after a few yards turn right on a lane that passes a large house with a tennis court and then, passing barns on the right, becomes a track for a mile to Hornton. Hornton is an impeccably neat village that is known for the local stone quarried near here.

Walk straight through the village, past the village green on your right with its stone cottages, and go northwards up the steep hill to a junction. Here go straight across, taking a track marked Poplars Farm. Beyond the farm follow the track, bearing left at a division of tracks and then through a field with a hedge on the right, veering round to a gap in the hedge and over a brook (the boundary between Oxfordshire and Warwickshire, *and which might prove difficult after very heavy rain*). Then proceed up the path bordered by trees and bear left across two fields, then go left again along a track on the ridge back to Ratley.

14

The Hidcotes and Ilmington Down

This walk over very undulating terrain visits the serene hamlets of Hidcote Boyce and Hidcote Bartrim and goes through Hidcote Combe. Ilmington Down above the beautiful village of Ilmington, with its Cotswold influence, is the highest point in Warwickshire.

Distance: 14 miles or 7 miles
Maps: Landranger 151; Pathfinder 1020/1021
Car Parking: Roadsides in Upper Quinton
Start/Finish: Upper Quinton (GR178464)
Refreshments: Pubs in Ebrington, Ilmington and Mickleton
Place of special interest: Hidcote Manor Garden (National Trust)
Shortened version: This walk follows a figure of eight route so can easily be shortened or divided into two shorter walks of approximately seven miles each by
A) Starting/finishing at Upper Quinton and passing through Mickleton, Hidcote Manor and Hidcote Combe
B) Starting/finishing at Ebrington (GR185400) (parking in side roads) and passing through Ilmington and Hidcote Manor. For this walk start reading from ➲ on page 62

ROM Upper Quinton village green take the lane southwards towards Meon Hill: the lane bears right and in a few yards go over a stile to follow a path waymarked Heart of England Way. Go straight across two meadows and in the third bear left to the top of the field; here turn right and walk with the hedge on the left, then with a hedge on the right in a fourth meadow.

Go straight across the fifth meadow, through a narrow strip of woodland, turn right for a few yards and then left, across the next field, and on the same heading through four more fields, swinging right in the fourth towards buildings. When level with them turn left down a narrow

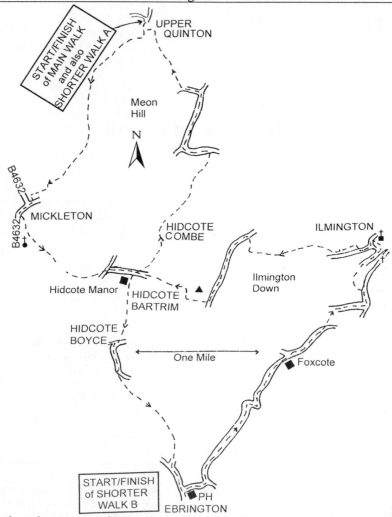

path and soon go right into a residential road (Meon Road) for about 300 yards and turn right into Mickleton along the road.

After about 200 yards turn left along a metalled drive that soon becomes a path and passes Mickleton church on the right. Go south-east across a meadow to reach a kissing gate. (*N.B. If you find yourself at a field gate carrying a Heart of England Way waymark you have gone a little too far to the right. Go left beside the hedge on your right to reach the kissing gate.*) Then from the kissing gate go straight ahead on a clear path to reach and cross a stile beside oak trees.

Ascend a sloping path bearing slightly right, then left in a second field to reach a gateway in the far left corner. Climb the next steep sloping meadow to the large gateposts of Kiftsgate Court Gardens (*open at advertised times*) at the top of the slope. Take the lane straight opposite (signed Hidcote Gardens). After about 300 yards turn right at the car park into Hidcote Bartrim – this in an attractive hamlet with thatched cottages.

If you are following the shorter walk A go straight across the car park and turn left on a waymarked path over a stile. Then continue from ✷ on page 63.

Hidcote Manor Gardens was given to the National Trust in 1948 by the great hoticulturalist Major Lawrence Johnson. It covers eleven acres and is made up of several small gardens each with a different theme, and was developed over a period of forty years. It is open to the public at advertised times.

✪ *Continue from here on shorter walk B.*

At the end of the village go through two gates and straight across two large fields on a clearly marked path to Hidcote Boyce – this is also a attractive village of traditional stone cottages.

Turn left at the first junction and left again a few yards further on, proceeding along a lane for a quarter of a mile: at a T-junction, signed Ebrington/Hidcote Bartrim, go right and then immediately left to take a path through a gate that goes through four fields with a hedge on the left to a lane. To the right is a good view of Chipping Campden and, on the

Looking down to Ilmington

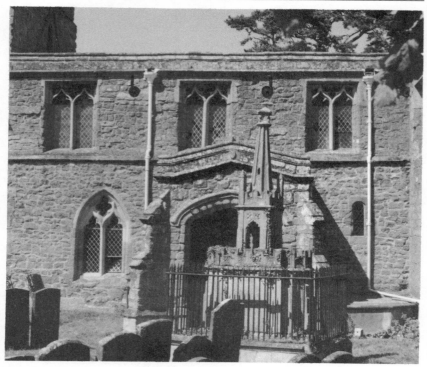

Church of St Mary, Ilmington

horizon, Broadway Tower. Over the lane go a few yards right and then keep on the previous heading across two fields, then along a track with a hedge on both sides to a road. Turn left into Ebrington.

➲ *Start here for the shorter walk B.*

Ebrington is a village of stone and thatch buildings built in sunken roads converging on a small green, shaded by three large oaks, close by the village inn and war memorial. It is known as 'Yabberton' by some locals.

Turn left at the triangular village green by the Ebrington Arms; at the end of the village, turn left (signed No Through Road) along the lane: the lane soon becomes a track; follow this for half a mile, then turn right along a stream and bear left after about 50 yards, soon to regain the original heading on the track to Foxcote House.

Just over a quarter of a mile on the lane beyond Foxcote take a path off left to climb to the ridge where you turn right on a bridleway with a wood on the right, to reach a lane. Turn left along the lane and after about 150 yards, where the lane curves to the right, pick up a path left that descends through a meadow and then through a gate along a green track, that becomes a track to Ilmington.

Ilmington is a beautiful stone village with a Cotswold influence, nestling at the foot of some of the steepest hills in Warwickshire.

From the village green take a path opposite St Philip's (Catholic) Church, adjacent to Daisy Cottage, which goes left through the churchyard of St Mary's (Anglican) Church to emerge on a lane. Turn left and soon right at a junction to climb a lane for about 150 yards to take a steep path (steps) on the right (marked Centenary Way and opposite Campden Hill Cottage).

Through trees go straight across the field, then turn left to walk with a hedge on the right; then (ignoring a hunter's gate marked 'Countryside Access Scheme') bearing right go over a stile to walk along a bridleway track that continues through several gates for about a quarter of a mile. Then on the same heading continue over two very undulating meadows to go through a gate and over a footbridge. Bear right through trees and then go straight up a sloping meadow and through a wood of young trees. When a track crossing the path through the wood is reached turn right.

Soon a field is reached; here swing left to go across the field to an unfenced lane and turn left for three quarters of a mile where radio masts are met.

Ilmington Down, at 854 ft, is the highest point in Warwickshire, close to the border with Gloucestershire. There are extensive views from here across the Vale of Evesham and the Cotswolds.

Turn right on a track that bears right and then left to descend to Hidcote Manor. Just before the car park is reached turn right on a path.

For the shorter walk B go straight across the car park and turn left on the lane to Hidcote Bartrim. Then continue reading from ✪ *on page 61.*

★ *Continue from here on shorter walk A.*

The path bears right across a meadow and then walk with a hedge on the left, then go straight across a large meadow, swinging left of some large sycamores and pines on the west facing slope.

Just past a large pine enter woodland, cross a stream (which may be dry) and go straight across a field into more woodland. Then bear left to cross a field and walk with a stream on the left for approximately half a mile to a lane and turn left. After a quarter of a mile turn right at a junction along the road for half a mile. Take a path on the left (Centenary Way), left of a bungalow, that goes along a drive, just past a small pool on the left, and then over a stile on the right, and then follows a clearly marked path over six fields and through a narrow copse of trees to go left across a small meadow and between cottages, back to Upper Quinton village green.

15

The Guitings

This walk is focused on the impressive Cotswold village of Guiting Power which is enviably situated above the Windrush Valley. The sloping village green is surrounded by traditional stone houses where the village bakery and post office still thrive. The route also zigzags through Guiting Woods and the villages of Temple Guiting and Kineton.

Distance: 13½ miles or 9 miles
Maps: Landranger 150/163; Pathfinder 1043/1067
Car parking: Roadsides, Wood Stanway or Temple Guiting
Start/Finish: Longer walk: Wood Stanway (GR063313); shorter walk: Temple Guiting (GR091278)
Refreshments: Pubs, Guiting Power and Kineton
Shortened Version: The walk can easily be shortened to 9 miles by starting and finishing at Temple Guiting (GR091278) thus eliminating the northern section. From the village walk south west from the church to the T-junction, turn right and then start reading from ✳ on page 67.

L EAVE Wood Stanway via the lane signed as a path to Hailes Abbey and Winchcombe, passing two of the old village water sources. The path then climbs with a hedge on the left, through a gate and along the left-hand edge of Hailes Wood for almost three quarters of a mile until the ancient earthwork of Beckbury Camp is reached.

Go right over a stile and bear diagonally right to follow a waymarked path over three meadows, swinging right in the second meadow, to reach a narrow lane and turn left to Farmcote, passing the small chapel of St. Faith . Continue on the lane for about half a mile until a junction of four tracks/lanes is reached and here turn right.

◎ *Rejoin here if you are following the shorter walk.*

Continue forward along the lane and in a quarter of a mile turn left at the next junction of lanes, and follow this narrow lane for approximately three quarters of a mile, then carry on along the same heading on the main

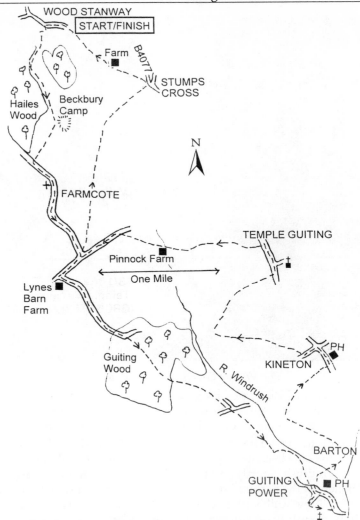

track (signed 'Wardens' Way') through Guiting Wood. When the main track bends sharply right, close to an old 'No Public Road' stone, go straight ahead on a narrow path on the fringe of the wood.

This path emerges from the wood to the right of a cottage. Continue straight ahead on a vehicle track for about half a mile and, at a bungalow by some barns, turn left down a slope and then bear right along a path through a copse, then past cottages into the village of Guiting Power.

From the village green turn right along the lane to the Parish Church

The Village Green, Guiting Power

of St. Michael which displays a good example of a Norman doorway. From the church door go left through a gate and straight across a field to a lane and turn left back to the village green, passing the Farmers Arms.

Turn right (down a lane marked 'No Through Road') and after about 100 yards the lane becomes a path with a hedge on the right and crosses the River Windrush. Shortly past the bridge go right over a stile, then walk with a hedge on the left to a corner and ahead to reach a stile in the fence on the left. Now walk with a wall on the right through two small fields to Little Windrush Farm and the hamlet of Barton.

At the end of the farm drive turn left along a narrow lane for just over half a mile and then take a path on the right which goes left of a cottage and through its garden, then through four fields with a hedge on the right (a wall in the fourth) to reach a lane: here turn left through the village of Kineton.

At the next crossroads turn left along a lane signed Roel Gate and Charlton Abbots for about 150 yards and then go right along a track with a narrow belt of woodland on its right-hand side, then with hedges on both sides until a metalled lane is reached. Here turn right to ascend the lane which climbs to the woods on the top of the hill. Then descend to a T-junction and turn left.

✻ *Start and end here for the shorter walk.*

Go straight on past Temple Guiting school. After about a quarter of a mile turn left through a gate beside a 'Public Footpath' stone onto a path running to the left of a private drive to 'Copperfields'. Follow this path with a fence on the right, then go through a gate into a copse of young trees. Leaving the copse walk with a fence on the left as it climbs a slope and then descends through woodland, keeping to the left-hand edge of the wood.

The path emerges from the woods by bearing left through a gate and along a slope for a few yards before going down to a gate. Turn right up a farm track which gradually curves to the left. Cross a lane and going through a gate immediately opposite walk straight ahead through a field and through a narrow strip of woodland to a lane. Turn left and after a

Chapel of St Faith

quarter of a mile a junction is reached (this spot was met earlier in the longer walk).

If you are taking the shorter walk now continue reading from ◎ *on page 64.*

Turn right to walk for two miles along a bridleway to Stumps Cross and the road (B4077). This long bridleway, Campden Lane, which has good views of the surrounding countryside was probably a medieval trackway used for the transportation of wool from Chipping Campden to Bristol for export. Note the fine line of venerable beech trees on the left as you approach the B4077. At the road the ancient stone is presumably all that remains of the original Stumps Cross.

Turn almost immediately off the B4077 on a path to the left, signed Cotswold Way. The path is not very distinct but it is clearly marked with Cotswold Way symbols. Follow these, being careful after going under power lines to the left of a large house to keep to the right-hand fence, then cross this over a stile. The path descends steeply through meadows, crossing some fine ridge and furrow, and then along a farm track to Wood Stanway and thus returns to your starting point.

16

The Westcotes and Icomb Hill

*Church Westcote and Nether Westcote are twin villages that nestle
gracefully on the western slopes of the broad Evenlode Valley. The walk
also takes in the quiet villages of Idbury and Icomb and climbs to Icomb
Hill and around Wyck Hill.*

Distance: 12 miles or 10 miles
Maps: Landranger 163; Pathfinder 1067/1068/1091
Car Parking: Roadsides by village green
Start/Finish: Wyck Rissington (GR192216)
Refreshments: Pubs at Nether Westcote and Bledington; café at
Nether Westcote
Shortened Version: The walk can be shortened to 10 miles by
taking the lane from Idbury Church to Bledington via Bould and
Foscote.

WYCK RISSINGTON is an old Saxon settlement on the east bank of
the River Dikler. It has a wide village green which is bordered
by seventeenth and eighteenth century cottages and features an
attractive duck pond. Gustav Holst, the British composer born in
Cheltenham and of Swedish descent, was the organist and choirmaster at
the parish church in 1892/93.

From Wyck Rissington take the path left that goes through the
churchyard of St Laurence parish church. Follow the Oxfordshire Way
signs as the path crosses a drive and then bears right across two fields, then
through a gateway into a third field, bearing slightly left through another
gateway (no gate) into a fourth field. Here walk with a hedge/trees on the
right up the slope until a waymark post is reached on the right: go through
a gap in the hedge and then continue on the same heading but with a hedge
on the left straight up the field, over a stile and through another field to a
lane.

There are good views from this lane near Wyck Beacon across to the
lakes around Bourton-on-the-Water. Turn right along this road for about

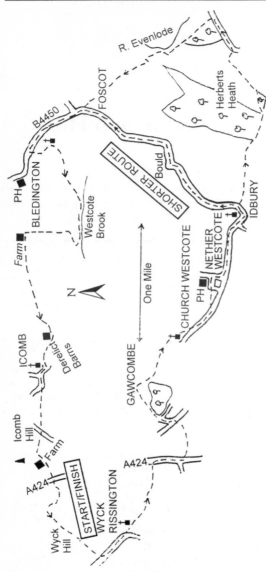

a quarter of a mile and opposite Court Hayes stables continue on the Oxfordshire Way path off left to the main road (A424).

Turn left for a few yards and then go right down a lane: when the lane turns to the right go straight on through the parkland of Gawcombe.

Go past farm buildings (with a dovecote) to swing right then left and take a path to the right opposite farm cottage No. 4: this path (no longer the Oxfordshire Way) descends, crosses a track, rises for about 50 yards, to then meet a division of ways.

Here take the left fork along a sunken track, emerging to reach a marker post. *At the time of writing the waymark signs had almost disappeared from this.* Here go left and downhill, noting the fine views to the left.

Cross a stream and go uphill, through a kissing gate (with stile) and continue on the same heading, following the waymarks. Reaching a large house keep left over stiles to emerge onto the driveway of the house. (*The footpath has been officially diverted here so does not correspond to the OS map*). Walk along the driveway to enter Church Westcote.

Go left along the lane passing the parish church, a phone box and a postbox on the right and in a few yards bear left across a greensward. Keep on the right of a wall and do not be diverted by a clearer track that goes back to the road. At the end of the wall continue forward for about 20 yards, fork left towards power poles and then cross three stiles to reach Nether Westcote and the New Inn.

Pass the New Inn and swing right up the lane and shortly at a junction turn left along a lane, continuing straight forward at a road junction (signed Foscot, Bledington, Kingham), to reach Idbury.

Idbury is a small village which affords good views of the Oxfordshire Cotswolds and the remains of the Forest of Wychwood. The Tudor manor house was once the home of Robertson Scott, the founder of the magazine *The Countryman*. There is an apt inscription over the door: 'Oh more than happy countryman if he knew his good fortune'.

If you are walking the shorter version continue along the lane past Idbury parish church: this eventually passes through the hamlet of Bould and then on to the village of Foscot. Then continue reading from ✳ on page 72.

Just beyond Idbury parish church take a signed bridleway through the gate on the right, descend the slope and go through a metal gate. Then immediately turn left to walk with a hedge on the left through two fields; then straight across two further fields and, in the next field, bear slightly right to a corner of a wood.

Turn left to walk walk with the wood (Herberts Heath) on the left along a signed bridleway. Eventually, at a junction of tracks, go left for about 40 yards, then at the next junction of tracks take the middle of three tracks which is a signed bridleway (blue waymark on post). Walk with a wood on the right and shortly, at a T-junction of tracks, turn left to walk with trees on the right. Shortly, upon reaching a crossroads of tracks, cross the main track and bearing slightly right over a cattle grid take the wide bridleway that is waymarked "d'Arcey Dalton Way".

Soon the way curves first to the right and, very shortly, to the left, passing over another cattle grid, still following the d'Arcey Dalton Way waymarks. After approximately 170 yards, where the wide track turns right, go straight on through a field with a hedge/trees on the right and soon, almost opposite a circle of pine trees, turn right to go through a gap in the hedge (waymark post) and straight across a field.

At the lane turn left: after just over a quarter of a mile turn left on a waymarked bridleway (Oxfordshire Way) to walk with a wood on the left (Cocksmoor Copse). Later pass through a gate into a wood. This wood is a County Naturalist Trust Nature Reserve. Continue on the path through the wood (this path can be very muddy!) for approximately a quarter of a mile to where a junction of routes is reached (waymark post). Here turn right, still following the Oxfordshire Way waymarks, to cross a field to a bridge over the River Evenlode.

Do not cross the bridge but turn left to walk with the river on the right until a concrete bridge is reached; here turn left on a clear track up the slope and soon turn right to walk along a grassy track with an open field and young plantations of trees on the right and a hedge on the left. Eventually, when a brook (Westcote Brook) is reached, turn left through a metal gate and in about 30 yards go over a cattle grid and through a gateway onto the lane and turn right.

★ *If you are following the shorter walk rejoin the main route here.*

At the next junction continue straight on along the road (B4450) to Bledington. Bledington, the largest village on the walk, has a spacious village green with a stream running through it and the cosy Kings Head Inn, oozing with fifteenth century character. Nearby is the lovely parish church which contains some Perpendicular windows with good stained glass.

If you wish to explore the village and visit its inn continue along the

Icomb from Icomb Hill

B4450. Otherwise turn left off the B4450 into Church Lane (signed Oxfordshire Way) to reach the parish church.

Take a waymarked path (Oxfordshire Way) through the graveyard, then with a fence, followed by a hedge on the right go through two fields. Go over a bridge over a stream, then bear left across two more fields: at the end of the second of these go right along the right bank of the Westcote Brook which you now follow for just over 200 yards.

After going through a hedge (where there is a concrete footbridge on the left) continue straight on for almost 100 yards, and opposite a wooden footbridge go diagonally right (following the blue waymark) up the field to a stile and gate in the far right corner.

Turn left up a track with a hedge on the right and a fence on the left for just over half a mile and then, shortly after passing Pebbly Hill Stud, turn left, before barns, on a signed path that goes straight across seven fields (crossing a track after the fifth), a distance of one mile. At this point turn left to walk around the boundary of an eighth field and go through a gate in the left-hand hedge. Then maintain the same heading through a gate past derelict barns on the right to ascend a clear track to Icomb. Turn right past the churchyard and left along the main street.

Icomb is a peaceful place with many attractive stone houses and cottages situated on the lower slopes of Icomb Hill (799 ft).

Where the lane turns to the right go left over a stile, taking a clear path that bears left (270 deg) to climb Icomb Hill and go through a gate between

Icomb village

the trees to bear left to the road. Go down the driveway to Hill Farm, straight on through the farmyard, and then left to follow the waymarked path running alongside a wall bordering a wood on the left, then turning right down a field with a hedge on the left to the main road (A424).

Cross the road carefully (fast traffic!) and follow a bridleway through a wood to a crossroads of tracks. Ignore the track on the left and bear slightly right to take the track with the blue bridleway waymark. At the next junction of tracks fork right along a signed bridleway that curves around Wyck Hill and then descends on a straight track to Wyck Rissington where you turn left to return to your car.

17

Cold Aston in the Cotswold Hills

Cold Aston, formerly known as Aston Blank, is appropriately named as the village lies exposed on high windswept hills. It is pleasantly clustered around its village green which has a large sycamore tree and the ancient Plough Inn. The walk also takes in the delectable hamlets of Compton Abdale, Hazelton and Notgrove with fine views from high on the wold.

Distance: 14 miles
Maps: Landranger 163; Pathfinder 1090
Car Parking: Roadside in Compton Abdale
Start/Finish: Compton Abdale (GR061167)
Refreshments: Pub, Cold Aston

S TARTING from the centre of the Compton Abdale, by the gate to the church, go north to ascend the steep lane through the village and after about a mile reach the main road (A40). Turn right for a few yards

A cold day in Cold Aston

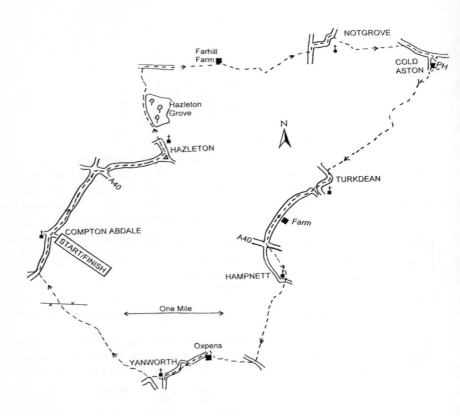

then take the lane on the left to Hazelton. At the beginning of the village ignore the first turning left by a large barn and take the second turning on the left, passing, after about 100 yards, a phone box.

Reaching a T-junction go left again to ascend the hill to the church. Keep on the same heading on a bridleway which soon keeps to the left hand boundary of the woodland of Hazelton Grove and then follows the right hand wall, then the left-hand wall, across two fields to a small copse and to a narrow lane: at the lane turn right and follow this lane for approximately one mile to Farhill Farm.

At the farm keep on the same heading down a sloping field to a gate at the bottom. Proceed right through the gate, then left through another gate and follow the track up to some barns. Go along the narrow lane for almost

300 yards to a T-junction, turn left, then first right, then first left, into the village of Notgrove.

From the village green turn right and proceed along the lane until the lane bears right: at this point take the field path left diagonally across the sloping meadow to a gate in the top right hand corner, go through the gate and proceed right to a narrow woodland on the left and walk through this narrow spur of attractive beech trees, so typical of the Cotswold landscape, which extends for about half a mile to a lane.

Turn right at the lane and walk into Cold Aston, passing the church on the left to an attractive cluster of houses at the village green where the Plough Inn is situated.

After refreshment proceed southwards from the village green for about 100 yards, branching right at the Y-junction, and then take the path on the right to go through two fields with a hedge on the right and emerge on the narrow lane/track to Turkdean (about 1½ miles distant). Turn left on this lane which drops steeply past Bang-up Barn and soon becomes a bridleway contouring downwards and then upwards to pass through a narrow belt of trees and then past a wood on the left to emerge at a T-junction. Turn left and go through Turkdean passing the church on the left.

Shortly, past the church, turn right down a steep narrow path, at the bottom passing a house on the left and crossing a ford to a lane at a bend. Go straight ahead uphill along the lane for approximately three quarters of a mile to reach the main road (A40). Cross the road, turn left, and after a few yards cross a stile on the right and walk diagonally across a field aiming to the left corner of a wall, then continuing forward on the same heading aiming to the left end of a belt of trees.

Go through a gate and in between farm buildings. We have now reached the quiet hamlet of Hampnett. Turn right for a few yards and then proceed down the track in a southerly direction. However, you may first wish to visit the small Norman Church of St George that you will see ahead of you. Of particular interest is the attractively, if somewhat unusually, painted chancel, the stencil decorations dating from 1868.

Continue down the track to reach a junction of tracks; here, turn left to climb the track to a road. Cross the road and proceed across a field with a wall on the right until a lane adjacent to a small reservoir is reached. Cross the lane and turn right on a path which cuts diagonally through a narrow, recently replanted, copse.

N.B. *At the time of writing the way through the copse was impassable and it was necessary to continue a few yards further forward and cross a stone stile on the right, then go forward to link up with the diagonal path.*

This problem has been reported and it is hoped that the correct way may be clear when you do this walk.

Go under electricity lines and across a gateway in the far corner on the field. Walk through the field with a fence on the right towards a group of cottages, and at the lane turn right, then left along a concrete track and, after a few yards, right, going through the yard of Oxpens Farm. Bear left to emerge on a narrow lane, passing Stowell Grove on the left hand side.

Follow the lane for about a quarter of a mile and where the lane turns to the right go over a stile on the left, taking the path which goes steeply down the 'hump' to rejoin the lane in the dip by the stream and climb to the hamlet of Yanworth. Shortly after passing Yarnworth church on the right a junction of tracks is reached; turn right taking the wide bridleway, which has fine views across the surrounding country side, for about two miles, branching left after about a mile. This will bring you to a lane which drops steeply back to Compton Abdale.

18

The Coberleys and Leckhampton Hill

The Cotswold hamlets of Coberley and Upper Coberley in the Upper Churn Valley are featured in this walk and there is a grand view of regency Cheltenham – the Cotswolds capital – from the Devil's Chimney on Leckhampton Hill.

Distance: 14 miles or 6 miles
Maps: Landranger 163; Pathfinder 1089
Car parking: disused quarry
Start/Finish: On lane, at disused quarry off B4070, three-quarters of a mile south of Leckhampton (GR946177)
Refreshments: Pubs, Seven Springs and Colesbourne
Shortened Version: This walk can easily be shortened to 6 miles by turning back to the start point from Coberley (GR962161)

FROM the car park turn left up the lane for about 75 yards and take the path on the left signed 'Cotswold Way' which runs along the edge of the scarp and climbs to the toposcope at the summit of Leckhampton Hill (952 ft) with its wide views. As you walk up to the summit keep to the edge of the scarp and you will soon see the Devil's Chimney – a limestone pinnacle formed by quarrymen when working the nearby quarries. Much of the stone used for building eighteenth and nineteenth century Cheltenham was obtained hereabouts.

From the toposcope walk east-south-east along the edge of the hill, immediately passing a wooden bench. Pass a trig point on your right to reach a kissing gate and a field gate. Don't go through these but swing left, then right through trees. At a T-junction of paths go right to pass a stone marker 'LECKHAMPTON HILL WALK 6'. Then follow a waymark and reaching the next Hill Walk marker continue forward, taking the lower path of two.

Follow the Cotswold Way signs (white circles), ignoring a bridleway

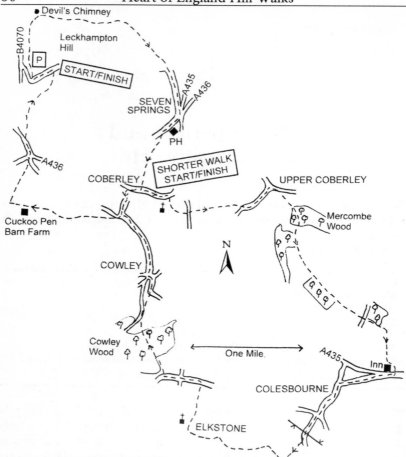

branching left. The path winds around and gradually down the hill and eventually enters a meadow with a hedge on the right. Go through this to bear left through a dell and then right along a broad track which joins a narrow lane to the main road (A435).

Turn right for a few yards, then right again along the A436 passing Seven Springs on the right. Opposite Sandford School take the path on the left which is clearly defined (fenced across meadow) and then with a hedge on the left into Coberley.

The twin villages of Coberley and Upper Coberley are pleasantly situated in the Upper Churn Valley near the source of the River Churn, a tributary of the Thames, at Seven Springs. Between the two settlements are the sites of the medieval villages.

If you are doing the shorter walk turn right at the T-junction (instead of left on the main walk) and shortly, at the next junction go left along the lane until a junction of lanes and a track are reached: here take the track opposite... (Now continue reading from ★ on page 83.)

At the small triangular village green with its old stone pillar, carrying the remains of a sundial, turn left, then left again at the T-junction and after about 200 yards reach on the right a large stone farmhouse. (Coberley Parish Church may be visited by using a gate in the farm wall and walking across a private garden.)

To continue the walk take a path on the right, next to the stone farmhouse which goes straight ahead through two fields and passes a pool on the left. Beyond the pool bear left across the field to a stile in the hedge, cross the road, and continue on the bridleway opposite, straight across a field, through a conifer plantation and woodland to emerge on a lane at Upper Coberley.

Walk straight on through the village and after about a third of a mile, at a junction of lanes, turn right for 50 yards and then fork right through a metal gate, to bear right across a field and through Mericombe Wood. Emerging from the wood take the left fork at a junction of tracks; this track is a very pleasant one along a ridge with mature beech trees on the right.

After three-quarters of a mile turn right to walk with a wood on the left, and shortly at a junction of tracks turn left along a wide track for half

The Devil's Chimney, Leckhampton Hill

Coberley. The ancient pillar on the village green

a mile, cross a lane and continue on the same heading through woods. Emerging from the wood turn right to walk at the edge of Colesbourne Park: about half way down the slope go through a metal kissing gate on the right and then walk with a hedge on the left and along a drive to the A435 at Colesbourne.

Turn right at the Colesbourne Inn along the main road for a few yards and take the left fork which, after half a mile, meets a junction. Turn left up the steep lane for half a mile to a junction under power lines; take the right fork (signed Beechpike 2, Winstone 3) and go straight ahead for about a quarter of a mile and then take a signed path on the right to walk with woods on the left to a lane and turn right.

After a few yards turn right again on a wide track: go straight ahead, ignoring a path to the right and a path to the left. After about three-quarters of a mile, and shortly past the path to the left, reach a bridlepath/RUPP sign. Follow this and shortly turn left at a signed junction of paths. At the next junction of tracks, go over a stile on the right and walk straight ahead to a lane at Elkstone.

Turn left to visit Elkstone Church, which is one of the finest Norman churches in the Cotswolds, with much architectural interest, including a Perpendicular west tower.

To resume the walk retrace your steps to the lane and continue until some new houses on the left are reached; here take a path that forks right and shortly, when a junction of tracks is reached, turn left at a path across a field. Approaching a lane bear right, away from the hedge, to reach the lane at a signed stone stile about 20 yards to the right of the left-hand corner of the field. Turn left and continue straight over a cross-roads for about a quarter of a mile to take a path on the right which goes left of a large barn and crosses two more stiles to descend through Cowley Wood on a waymarked path.

When a junction of tracks is reached bear right along the main track for about 60 yards and then take an easily missed, narrow secluded path on the right. This climbs through trees and goes over a stile and straight across a field to a narrow lane. Turn right for about 100 yards and then go right on a path that bears left through the parkland of Cowley Manor, a nineteenth century Italianate mansion, to a lane.

Turn left along the lane and then left again at the next junction in Cowley village. Take the right fork at the following junction, go along this road for about 50 yards, then turn right along a narrow lane for three-quarters of a mile and at a junction of lanes turn left on a track...

★ *Continue from here for the shorter walk.*

...and shortly take the right fork to pass Cuckoopen Barn Farm. Note the plaque at the entrance to the farm that records the building of 'the world's biggest straw rick' in 1982.

Shortly past the farm turn right on a track descending to the A436. Cross the road and take the lane, passing a golf club on the right before turning right on a path signed 'Cotswold Way'. Follow this for three-quarters of a mile to the road and turn left to return to the car park.

Index

Also from Meridian…

THE MONARCH'S WAY
by Trevor Antill

A new long distance walk that closely follows the route taken by Charles II after his defeat by Cromwell's forces at Worcester in 1651. Visiting many historic places, perhaps previously known to readers only through the history books, it also goes through some of the finest scenery in western and southern England.

Book 1: Worcester to Stratford-upon-Avon. 175 miles.
ISBN 1 869922 27 1. £5.95. 112 pages. 19 photographs, 8 drawings, 19 maps. Paperback.

Book 2: Stratford-upon-Avon to Charmouth. 210 miles.
ISBN 1 869922 28 X. £6.95. 136 pages. 21 photographs. 23 maps. Paperback.

Book 3: Charmouth to Shoreham. 225 miles.
ISBN 1 869922 29 8. £6.95. 136 pages. 21 photographs. 25 maps. Paperback.

IN THE FOOTSTEPS OF THE GUNPOWDER PLOTTERS
by Conall Boyle

When the Gunpowder Plotters failed to blow up Parliament they fled, visiting their houses in Warwickshire and Worcestershire. In this unique guide you can follow their trail – by car, by bicycle, or on foot.
ISBN 1 869922 23 9. £4.95. 96 pages. 13 drawings. 19 maps. Paperback.

FAVOURITE WALKS IN THE WEST MIDLANDS
by members of the Birmingham CHA Rambling Club
Edited by Tom Birch and Mary Wall

A collection of twenty-two attractive walks from members of one of Birmingham's oldest walking clubs.
ISBN 1 869922 26 3. £4.95. 112 pages. 24 photographs. 23 maps. Paperback.